WANTED

SONG OF SOLOMON 7:10

ANGELA MORGAN

WestBow
PRESS®
A DIVISION OF THOMAS NELSON
& ZONDERVAN

WestBow Press books may be ordered through booksellers or by contacting:

WestBow Press
A Division of Thomas Nelson & Zondervan
1663 Liberty Drive
Bloomington, IN 47403
www.westbowpress.com
844-714-3454

Scripture taken from the King James Version of the Bible.

ISBN: 978-1-6642-8606-1 (sc)
ISBN: 978-1-6642-8605-4 (e)

Library of Congress Control Number: 2022922523

Print information available on the last page.

WestBow Press rev. date: 12/19/2022

Jesus,

You're the One my heart longed for before I even knew it could long for anything. You're the One who was always meant for me, and yet I sought others to fill that void. When I realized I needed You, it was then that I had a want for You, and even after all these years, I long still. May I never lose the wonder.

Yours forever,
Angela

In dedication to …

My children—Brianne, Justin, and Levi—
and daughter-in-love, Hannah

I thank God that He allowed me to be your mom and mother-in-law. I love
you. You are wanted and loved deeply by Jesus. Know *whose* you are!

CONTENTS

FOREWORD

The first time I met Angela Morgan, let me tell you—I could see God in her. It was Spring 2019 at a women's ministry luncheon. It was outdoors, and there were other people there, but there was an immediate bond when we sat down next to one another. There was an immediate connection. It was palatable. It was a Jesus connection.

From that moment forward, Angela and I were connected like sisters in Christ. I don't know how else to explain it. I just *knew* she was a true warrior and a godly woman.

This book, *Wanted*, is a study laden with scripture, but it is actually much more than that. Its purpose is made clear in her letter to her readers. In it Angela tells you that you have a divine appointment with God. He has placed you here as proof that you are wanted passionately by Jesus Christ.

You are. So am I. It is our privilege to have this book in our hands—and it's easy to realize why.

Angela's story, as told from the perspective of the woman at the well in John 4, is nothing short of remarkable and inspired. Before I began reading this book, I knew Angela to be anointed with her knowledge of God's Word, but now I believe I have never met a woman who knows scripture in the same way she does.

Like the woman at the well, Jesus came to Angela while she was a sinner. Angela writes, "Coming out of one broken marriage and walking into another that is barely hanging on by a thread, I ask myself these questions. This cannot be what life is like, right? How do people live with such passion and love for Christ? I didn't understand it, but I knew I was willing to at least try to figure it out."

While the way Angela relates her life to that of the woman at the well is amazing, her insights into other areas of the Bible are just as incredible. In her breakdown of the Song of Solomon 7:10, for example, Angela examines the words *beloved* and *desire* with pinpoint detail and wisdom.

She then emphasizes, "Jesus wants You. I know many of us struggle with the insecurities of not being 'good enough' or 'doing enough,' and in return it will leave us empty … I believe there are moments in our lives when we get so busy in the doing that we forget why we do what we do. We have many relationships in this world, but none come close to the relationship with Christ Himself."

I have been saved since 2013—and *Wanted* has lit a fire in my spirit. I could literally sense God's presence as I read it over two days. I did it that way on purpose. I didn't want to just read it straight through, so I took time to process everything she had written. I'm so glad I did. It gave me chill bumps because *Wanted* is that personal and intimate. It has refreshed me and helped me to have a more intimate walk with Jesus.

As I read and reflected, I couldn't help but think, *My goodness. Who are the folks in my life I could give this to?* That question has given me a passion to take *Wanted,* get a group of women together, and walk them through it. Why? It is that powerful! They will see God in a different light.

Since I read *Wanted,* God has communicated so much to me about my life and relationship with Him. He's told me we are never too old. It doesn't matter where we are in our walk with Him. *God wants us.* As long as we are focused on Him and keep our eyes on Him, everything else is second place. We can have an intimate relationship with Him through prayer and worship by getting in His Word.

At the end of *Wanted,* there is a story I don't want you to miss. It's about a woman named Shawn, whom I just happened to have met in person at a small group study. I won't give away her surprising story, but let me just say that *Wanted* has changed her life. Once she met Jesus at the well of decision in her life, she accepted Him as her Lord and has never looked back. Do not miss this story!

I know the calling God has on Angela's life. He is using her in such a powerful way to bring people closer to Him. She is an awesome servant. She inspires me, and she will inspire you.

Read on—and you'll never be the same again.

Jeannie Lynch
Author, *Don't Quit Five Minutes Before the Miracle Happens*
Cofounder, No Limit's Women Conferences, LLC
Private Practice Therapist, LPC-S, NCC, LLC, in Decatur, Alabama

PREFACE

To the Reader,

I believe it's a divine appointment that you are here. You have been prayed for. A holy anticipation wells up in my soul because of the truth that you are wanted passionately by Jesus Christ. With deep gratitude, I say thank you for being here. I am humbled and grateful. My prayer is not only that the truths from this study will take you from being a child of God but also that you will walk as a radiant bride of Christ, one who is passionately in love with Jesus Christ and waiting for His glorious return.

Years ago I realized my identity isn't found in me, what I *do* in this life, or even what I am for Jesus, but it is found solely in Him and Him alone. Honestly, there will never be enough words on this side of heaven that will be able to express the thankfulness I have in knowing that Jesus saw me in all my filth and chose to sanctify, wash, and redeem my life and make it His. The truth is, my life and the choices I made at a younger age and into my adulthood were disgusting, and unforgivable to many. It is so good to remember what Christ has redeemed us from. Going down the memory lane of my life will always leave me amazed at how very much I am unworthy of Him and how very much He loves us.

So, here we go …

I am one of the fabulous four favorite daughters of Bobby and Becky Bonner. I was born in Corpus Christi, Texas, on July 3, 1975. My mom and dad were high school sweethearts and married soon after. Dad was given a scholarship to play baseball at Texas A&M University. His amazing talent landed him a short-stop position to play for the Baltimore Orioles. He was with them for a few years, but at the age of twenty-eight years old, he walked away from it all and surrendered to go to Zambia, Africa, to be a missionary.

My parents' personal testimonies of how Jesus changed their lives are amazing. If you would like to know more about their story, you can order my dad's book, *From the Diamond to the Bush*. It is incredible! In all honesty, my parents love Jesus. I'm not just saying that because I know they will read this. It has always been evident, as long as I have been alive, in total surrender, in their talk, in their walk at home, and everywhere else. They are solid, and many would call

them both the "real deal." In fact, my whole life my dad has taught me that there are two times to pray, read your Bible, and go to church: when you feel like it and when you don't. And if we whined about it, he told us to rub some dirt on it and get back in the game.

When my dad walked away from "the show" at twenty-eight years old to surrender to the mission field, I was shocked. I was old enough to remember the feeling of it all. I didn't understand why he would walk away from baseball, let alone go to a foreign field where people knew absolutely nothing about the sport, then take his wife and four daughters over there. Wow! Nonetheless, we embarked on that journey of total faith. I was fourteen when we went to Zambia, Africa, and I certainly wasn't happy about it.

Many things happened in Africa that I will take with me forever, but there is one memory that has stuck with me for years. One kid, in particular, born without legs, crawled to the church gathering held yearly at the Kafulafuta Mission. When I asked how far he had crawled, I was told one mile. Wow. One mile. This boy, about twelve years old, crawled just to sit on the ground in the hot sun for hours of preaching and teaching from the Word of God. By the way, he had a smile on his face from ear to ear. I was sixteen at the time and so mesmerized by his story that I questioned what made people do stuff like that.

I adapted as well as I knew how there on the mission. I made friends and over time met another missionary kid. Chris was also from Texas. We both moved back to the States, I graduated from high school in June, turned eighteen in July, and was married to him on July 17. We moved to a small town in Texas. I was so independent and wanted what I wanted. I remember crying for two weeks straight after leaving my parents. I had no idea what I had just gotten myself into. But no one could have stopped me from marrying him or doing whatever I wanted to do. I was one stubborn eighteen-year-old.

Just as with any new thing, it takes a bit to adjust or adapt. It was a definite culture shock for me. But I pulled up my bootstraps and got a job at a video store in the small town of Kirbyville, Texas.

After a while, I began to go into a dark depression with feelings of unworthiness and not being wanted or needed by anyone. My family and sisters were back in Zambia. They didn't need me. My husband didn't need me. My friends didn't need me. You know all those lies the enemy gets us to believe. I caved and several times began contemplating taking my life, but I believe the Lord isn't willing that any should perish. God frustrated mine and the enemy's plans to take my life when I found out I was pregnant with my firstborn daughter, Brianne. Someone needed me. Oh, how she was and still is my saving grace!

God used her to start my journey to Him, but it wouldn't be quick. Remember, I told you I was stubborn. Over time I grew bored. I became bored with being married. I got bored with being a housewife. I walked away and began to accept all the invitations from friends to house parties. By the way, nothing good happens at those things. Nothing. A few years of this lifestyle opened up a door for me to have an affair and cheat on my first husband. Our sin doesn't just affect us. Nobody deserves the pain I caused and I walked away from my first marriage.

Micheal and I met on February 15, 1998. I fell head over heels madly in love with this man, who came home from the marine corps and went straight into my heart. We have been together ever since. I'm not about to tell you this was a fairy-tale union. We fought a lot. I was pregnant with our first child, Justin, and we soon moved to Katy, Texas.

I shared about my parents and the testimony of their total devotion to Christ, so it's safe to say I knew what it meant to be a Christian. I knew what it was supposed to *look* like anyway—to be dragged to church every time the doors were opened. To be honest, while I was growing up, the desire that my parents had to pursue Jesus was never really there for me personally. Don't get me wrong—I was definitely trying hard to do all the right things, to look the part. You know, the American churchy Christian.

Micheal and I and our two kids, Brianne and Justin, were now living in the new town of Katy, Texas. We started faithfully going to church, I started singing in the choir, and I joined a few Bible studies. But I still longed for something that was missing. I found myself falling deeper into sin and condemnation, never measuring up, fighting with Micheal all the time, and surely never feeling like I was a Christian. All these things paralyzed me with guilt and shame. Seriously I felt like such a failure, going from one broken marriage, and walking into another that was daily barely hanging on by a thread. I asked myself the questions that had started so long ago when I was sixteen in Zambia. *What makes people walk miles to hear the preaching of the Word of God? Surely there is more to this life! How do people live with such passion and love for Christ?* I didn't understand it, but I knew I was willing to at least try to figure it out. I mean, what did I have to lose at this point? I was twenty-eight years old, divorced, and struggling in another marriage with two kids.

It was about midnight on August 16, 2003, when all those questions were stirring in my heart. I couldn't stand it any longer. I fell on my knees in my living room floor, yelling at God. "What makes people live for You, give up everything to go to a foreign country, and be completely sold out for You? What is the driving force, the passion behind it? What makes people die for You? Walk away from Major League Baseball and go to a foreign country for You?"

I was alone, trembling, and weeping on my face in my living room. The house was so quiet. My family was sleeping. I heard Him. I heard Him for the first time in my life. It was like Jesus was whispering to my heart to get to know Him. I could hardly move. But Bible in hand, I opened it up, and it fell to John 4. I looked down and read these beautiful words: "If thou knewest the gift of God, and who it is that saith to thee, Give me drink; thou wouldest have asked of him, and he would have given thee living water" (John 4:10).

That was the first time in my whole existence that His Word came alive to me. In this verse, Jesus answered my questions. He said that if I knew Him, not just about Him, I would understand why people give up everything for Him. On that summer night in Katy, Texas, I heard Him. I saw Him. I called on the name of Jesus and was born again, and I have never gotten over Him. Confession became natural in His presence. I gave it to Him, and He gave me Himself, the Living Water. What kind of trade is that? I weep even now while typing this.

Just a few months later, on December 5, 2003, my husband, Micheal, was born again. This adventure we have been on has been nothing short of miracle after miracle and glory to glory. Has it been easy? No. There have been a lot of trials and struggles along the way, moments when I wanted to throw in the towel. But Jesus and all His sovereignty and forgiveness has been with me at every step, in every moment, through every trial, and in every pain. He has never left me, and it was in those moments that I got to know Him even more. What a Savior! My deep desire is that you will get to know the Jesus I know. He has forgiven me of so much. My prayer is that, no matter what you have done in your past or what you are currently in now, that you would know Jesus wants you. Right where you are, let Him in. Call on His name. Friend, He loves you. He wants you, and He is worth your all.

Two Times,

Angela ♡

ACKNOWLEDGMENTS

I thank my God upon every remembrance of you.

To my husband, Micheal Morgan, who has always encouraged me to get *Wanted* finished. For years you have wiped tears from my eyes and spoken God's Word into my soul to keep me going for Jesus. I'll never forget the day you picked me up off the floor in our hallway and said, "God hasn't forgotten you, Angela. His Word to you will never return void, it will be accomplished, and it will prosper." I couldn't have done this without you, nor would I want to. I love you! Thank you.

To my parents, Bobby and Becky Bonner, who encourage me to follow Jesus no matter what. You have always taught me that there are two times to praise Him, two times to pray, and two times to read your Bible: when you feel like it and when you don't. Thank you for your persevering passion for Christ. It sharpens me. I love you both so much!

To my family in Lufkin, Texas: Natalie Nichols, Joel and Teresa Wier, Aran Greene, Natalie Jansen, and Misti and Spence Peppard. You have taught me the value of the prayer closet before the platform. Thank you for worshipping Jesus authentically and for teaching me that your praise is the overflow of your worship to Him. Thank you for the all-night prayers to the One you're doing it all for. I miss and love you all.

To Shawn Hager, my sister in Christ, for using your talents for Jesus. Thank you for always encouraging me in His Word and graciously helping me pen *Wanted* to paper. Words fail me for the countless hours I know you have put in to make this happen. Thank you for weeping with me at the feet of Jesus. Sister, your friendship is a rare treasure and an example of Jesus to my life. I am eternally grateful for you. Your love for Him is breathtaking, and many lives are being changed because of it. Thank you with all my heart. I love you— mean it!

To Bethany Cuevas, my sister in Jesus. I am blown away by the breathtaking beauty of your designs. When the Lord gave me the vision for *Wanted*, I saw these ideas in my heart and mind. Thank you for drawing the powerful simplicity of truth and being so gracious in allowing them to be in this book. There is no doubt in my mind that each piece will speak a message words simply cannot. I am honored to have your artwork in *Wanted*. I love you!

To Jeannie Lynch, my energetic, passionate-for-Jesus, loving sister in Christ. I will never forget the day God orchestrated our paths to cross at Mellow Mushroom. You have been a constant truth speaker in my life, illuminating the narrow path and pushing me to keep my eyes on the face of Jesus, because He is worthy of it all. Your love for Christ is a beautiful thing to behold, and it is so sharpening to my life. I am forever grateful for you, sister. Your rewards are great in heaven. I love you!

Thank you to every woman over the years who sat with me as the Holy Spirit taught us through this study. Your support, prayers, and presence have encouraged me beyond what my words could ever describe. I am humbled to have been given the opportunity to share these precious moments at His feet with you.

INTRODUCTION

I would tell you my name, but it doesn't really matter who I am. However, I must tell you the thing that happened to me because it has changed my life forever!

The day started like any other day. Nothing was special or out of the ordinary as I made my way through the city to draw water from Jacob's well. As I drew closer, I noticed a man sitting on the well, as if He were waiting to meet someone there. The closer I got, I realized He was a Jew, which caused me to hesitate. You see, I am a Samaritan, and the Jews hate Samaritans. But there was something different about this man.

I was cautiously walking up to the well when He suddenly spoke to me. "Give me a drink."

I trembled.

I tried to show my brave side as I answered Him, "Why are You speaking to me? You are a Jew, and Jews have nothing to do with Samaritans."

His gaze never broke from me. His voice was tender and gentle, and there was no hate or disgust etched on His face as He answered, "If you knew the gift of God and who it is who talks with you, you would ask of Him, and He would have given you Living Water."

I will admit His answer to my question left me confused. I didn't quite understand what He meant. As I looked around, I saw He had no pot to draw water, and the well was deep. Before I knew it, I asked Him, "Where do You get this Living Water? For You have nothing to draw with. Are You greater than our father Jacob who gave us this well?"

Without hesitation, He confidently said, "Whosoever drinks of this water will thirst again, but whosoever drinks of the water that I shall give him shall never thirst, but the water I shall give him shall be in him a well of water springing up into eternal life."

"Sir," I exclaimed, "give me this water so that I may never thirst again! So that I will never have to come back to this place to draw water!" I was expecting Him to hand me a cup or waterpot, but that isn't what happened. He began asking questions, personal questions. He

spoke to me about my past, my sins, things secret and kept hidden. How did He know? I was amazed. "Surely, you are a prophet!" I proclaimed.

He continued to speak to me and told me about God seeking those who would worship Him in Spirit and in truth. I told Him I had heard of God and the stories about His greatness. I knew the Messiah would one day come, and when He did, He would tell us all things. He would tell us truth.

That's when it happened. He spoke these words into the depths of my soul. They pierced my heart and melted me to the core. "I who speaks with you am He."

I was breathless, speechless. The Messiah, the Christ, was speaking to *me*. He knew all I had ever done, yet He chose to speak to me. As soon as He said who He was, the men who traveled with Him returned to the well. I am sure they must have been surprised to see me there as they stared toward me. But it didn't matter. He never looked away from me, and I couldn't turn my eyes from His.

"Others need to know! Everyone needs to know who it is that sits at the well!" I whispered to myself. I smiled as I began to turn away, and I ran as fast as I could back into the city. I couldn't hide the joy and freedom pouring out from within me as I stopped every person I saw, telling him or her about my encounter with the Messiah at the well. "Is not this the Christ? For He told me all the things I have ever done! Come! See Him for yourself!"

It wasn't long before many came out of the city to meet this man. Everyone gathered around Him and believed on Him, not just because of what I had said about Him but because they were able to meet the Christ Jesus, the Messiah, for themselves. Jesus stayed with us for two days, and we all marveled at His words, His truth.

I will never forget the day I met the man who told me all that I have ever done, yet He still wanted to know me and allow me the gift of knowing Him. He filled the longings of my soul and my heart when He gave to me Living Water. And He has been true to His Word; I have never once thirsted for anything ever again, for He has satisfied me to overflowing.

I extend the same invitation to you as I did to those of the city that day. Come! See for yourself the Christ, the Messiah, and taste of His Living Water. You will see that He is good.

P.S.

If you are still wondering about my name, I will tell you this … Jesus changed it and gave me His. You see, I am my Beloved's, and He is mine, and His name is the only one that matters.

CHAPTER 1

i am His

INVITATION

In this was manifested the love of God toward us, because that God sent his only begotten Son into the world, that we might live through him. (1 John 4:9)

We love him, because he first loved us. (1 John 4:19)

The relentless pursuit of our Savior begins before we ever realize we need Him. He will do and use anything to draw us to Himself. There are many examples of the evidence of this truth woven throughout my life, but one of the most precious examples of this was in 1994 before I was saved.

I had reached a very low and dark place in my life. A lot of life's poor and wrong choices were starting to stack up, and I had reached a breaking point. I began to look around and buy into the lie that no one needed me. My first husband didn't need me. My parents were in Africa as missionaries; they didn't need me. And my job needed me only to perform the tasks at hand, but the people there didn't really care for me as a person.

Anyone could have taken my place. I began to consider suicide as an option and soon put a plan together to take a bottle of pills, go to sleep, and never wake up. During this contemplation of taking my life, I became violently sick to my stomach, and my coworker asked me if I was pregnant. At first, I denied it, but eventually I took a pregnancy test. Sure enough, I found out I was pregnant with my beautiful daughter, Brianne. Nine years before I met Jesus in Katy, Texas, He was pursuing me and using my daughter to spare my life. I am so thankful He did.

I am my beloved's, and his desire is toward me. (Song of Solomon 7:10)

Beloved: Darling, dear, precious, cherished, treasured, prized.

Desire: To want, a strong feeling of want.

Jesus wants You. I know that many of us struggle with the insecurities of not being good enough or doing enough; in return, they leave us feeling empty and give us feelings of being unwanted. The purpose of this study is to remind you that it's not all about what He wants from you but that He simply wants you. Through His Word, prayer, and meeting together, may you come to the reality that Calvary was never intended for you to come to the knowledge of a robotic religion. It's a deep-rooted and intimate relationship. All of us start off good, but for some reason, we wind up falling into the cookie-cutter religious mentality and then wonder why we are so empty. Numb. The truth is, our lack of motivation and passion for Christ is a direct reflection of our lack of Christ's love in us.

For the love of Christ constraineth us. (2 Corinthians 5:14)

Constraineth: To hold together with constraint. To press together
with the hand. To hold together lest it fall to pieces or something
fall away from it.

> The beloved of the Lord shall dwell in safety by him; and the Lord shall cover
> him all the day long, and he shall dwell between his shoulders. (Deuteronomy
> 33:12)

Wow. Talk about a holy hug from heaven! Here is the truth: Jesus Christ is the Living Word.
And the Word is God. God is love.

> In the beginning was the Word, and the Word was with God, and the Word
> was God … And the Word was made flesh, and dwelt among us, (and we beheld
> his glory, the glory of the only begotten of the Father,) full of grace and truth.
> (John 1:1, 14)

> And we have known and believed the love that God hath to us. God is love;
> and he that dwelleth in love dwelleth in God, and God in him. (1 John 4:16)

I believe there are moments in our lives when we get so busy in the *doing* that we forget
why we do what we do. We have many relationships in this world, but none come close to the
relationship with Christ. Until we walk in that reality, we will wind up feeling empty every
single time.

God designed and created us to have a longing for deep intimacy with Him. Nothing and
no one else will ever fulfill that longing. Until we connect with that purpose, we will never be
satisfied.

> Could today be the day I see my Jesus's face?
>
> To look upon the One who took my sinful place?
>
> The beautiful moment when our eyes meet,
>
> Remembering the times I sat at His feet.
>
> What a glorious day it will be
>
> To ever live in His presence and the things I will see!
>
> My one true desire from my heart to declare
>
> Is to bow at His feet with no more despair.

You see, I have a *love*; He died for me.

So until He returns, this life is His that you see.

—Angela Morgan

Love not the world, neither the things that are in the world. If any man love the world, the love of the Father is not in him. (1 John 2:15)

Jesus told us that He came that we might have life and have it more abundantly (John 10:10). The words "more abundantly" simply mean plentifully; extremely; in large quantities; an abundant supply of. Sisters, let's get to know Him.

CHAPTER 2

THE WORD, THE WELL, AND THE WOMAN

THE WORD

So where do we start? The Bible answers that question.

> In the beginning was the Word, and the Word was with God, and the Word was God. (John 1:1)

> And the Word was made flesh, and dwelt among us. (John 1:14)

We start in the beginning. And in the beginning was the Word, who is Jesus. Anything and everything that ever was, is, and ever will be began with Jesus, who is God and who was with God. This study is centered on John 4, but we can't miss the significance of the first three chapters leading up to it. So, let's take a brief walk through these chapters to lay the foundation of our journey together.

Our Jesus is a romantic. John 1 is where Jesus steps out of heaven into this world and introduces Himself to us as the Word. The Son of God, who always was and forever will be, the Creator of all, just entered the scene to pursue a love relationship with you and me. Think about this for a second. The Bible says Jesus Christ is Alpha and Omega, the Beginning and End. He is the Creator of time itself and is not bound by it, yet here He is, stepping into time for you and me. He restores to us the broken relationship between God and humanity that was lost because of the curse of sin back in the Garden of Eden.

> Therefore, behold, I will allure her, and bring her into the wilderness, and speak comfortably unto her. (Hosea 2:14)

> For the Son of man is come to seek and to save that which was lost. (Luke 19:10)

John 2 records the first miracle of Jesus: turning water into wine at a wedding. He could have done anything and picked any place to perform His first miracle, and He chose a wedding. Coincidence? Nope. It's safe to say our Jesus had a wedding on His mind. He had His bride on His mind, too. John 2 shows us who Jesus is. We are getting to know about Him, including His character and values. He was coming to break religious tradition. After His first miracle, Jesus entered the temple, which we will dive into in the upcoming chapters.

> And I will give her her vineyards from thence, and the valley of Achor for a door of hope: and she shall sing there, as in the days of her youth, and as in the day when she came up out of the land of Egypt. (Hosea 2:15)

Throughout scripture, "wine" or "fruit of the vine" represents joy. Jesus came to offer us a pure joy only He could give—not just a moment of happiness every now and then but Himself. This never-ending supply of pure joy is in, by, and through a personal, intimate relationship with Him. Even in the hardest and darkest of times, there will be a song in the night He has placed in your heart and a joy you simply can't explain except that it is Jesus! Just Jesus.

John 3 starts off with the conversation with Nicodemus that "you must be born again." God gave us the greatest gift, His Son, Jesus Christ. I don't know about you, but when I started to see who Jesus was and compared it to who I was, I began to think there was no way I could approach Him. There was no way I would be someone He would want to look at, let alone want a relationship with. Right on cue, anticipating these hesitations that would come, Jesus tells us all that is required to have a relationship with Him. Check it out:

> For God so loved the world, that he gave his only begotten Son, that whosoever believeth in him should not perish, but have everlasting life. (John 3:16)

> And I will betroth thee unto me for ever; yea, I will betroth thee unto me in righteousness, and in judgment, and in lovingkindness, and in mercies. I will even betroth thee unto me in faithfulness: and thou shalt know the Lord. (Hosea 2:19–20)

Betroth: To promise or pledge one to be the future spouse of another. To contract to anyone. A man is betrothed to a lady.[1]

John 3 ends with John speaking of our Lord and Savior as the Bridegroom. He could have used any other name here to describe who our Jesus is. He could have repeated that Jesus was the Lamb of God. He could have called Him the Savior of the world or the King of kings and Lord of lords. The possibilities are endless when it comes to who our Savior is, but he spoke of Him and saw Him as the Bridegroom. It was in this description of Jesus that John said his joy was fulfilled. Now that, precious one, is a powerful statement. Don't miss what is being said here. The bride of Christ, the church, you and I were on the Lord's mind, so much so that John the Baptist referred to Jesus as the Bridegroom.

At a wedding, two people stand out in the crowd. It doesn't matter whether you know anyone at the wedding; you can always tell who the bride and the groom are. But it isn't only because of how they are dressed. Their whole countenance and attitude are different from everyone else's. They know that today everything changes. The waiting is over. That is what John saw in our Jesus here—a Bridegroom excited and anticipating His bride.

He that hath the bride is the bridegroom: but the friend of the bridegroom, which standeth and heareth him, rejoiceth greatly because of the bridegroom's voice: this my joy therefore is fulfilled. (John 3:29)

To better understand the truths of John 4, we need to look at a brief historical background.

THE WELL

Now Jacob's well was there. Jesus therefore, being wearied with his journey, sat thus on the well: and it was about the sixth hour. (John 4:6)

Wells are very significant in the Word of God. In historical Hebrew culture, they are symbolic and represent new beginnings and creation; they are *life giving*. Typical Hebrew history shows that wells are places of betrothal scenes. When a Jewish man and a woman met at a well, a wedding usually followed. Don't take my word for it; take God's. In Genesis 24:10–27, Abraham sent his servant to find a wife for his son, Isaac. In Exodus 2:15–22, Moses met his wife Zipporah at a well when she came to water her father's flock.

But notice this: the well Jesus was sitting on wasn't just any well; it was Jacob's well. In Genesis 29, it was at this exact well and at the same time of day when Jacob met his wife, Rachel. Jesus wasn't there by coincidence; this was a divine, purposeful, detailed meeting. He was there looking for a bride.

Look at John 1:1, 14 with me again.

In the beginning was the Word, and the Word was with God, and the Word was God … And the Word was made flesh, and dwelt among us. (John 1:1, 14)

I am Alpha and Omega, the beginning and the ending, saith the Lord, which is, and which was, and which is to come, the Almighty. (Revelation 1:8)

Jesus was there when Jacob met Rachel. He was there when Israel and Samaria parted ways, becoming enemies of each other, because He was *in the beginning*, and He *is the Beginning*. The Word always was, is, and forever will be. And it is because Jesus knew the value and importance of this specific location that He chose Jacob's well. Everything the Lord does has purpose and meaning. The disciples knew what this well represented to the Jews. The Samaritans also understood the impact of His presence there.

THE WOMAN

> He left Judea, and departed again into Galilee. And he must needs go through
> Samaria. Then cometh he to a city of Samaria, which is called Sychar, near to
> the parcel of ground that Jacob gave to his son Joseph. (John 4:3–5)

Judea is south of Galilee, and between them is Samaria. The size of Samaria is forty miles north to south and thirty-five miles east to west. The Samaritans were ancestral enemies of the Jews, who hated them so much that they traveled around the land of Samaria to avoid any contact. But here we discover that Jesus "must needs go through Samaria." Jesus, a Jew, was going against tradition, religion, and understanding by just stepping into Samaria. But He didn't just cross over the border; He went to Sychar. Sychar is located twenty miles deep into Samaria, right in the middle. This wasn't just a few-hours'-journey-to-touch-base-and-leave type of visit our Lord was making. It was a committed, purposeful, divine mission with nothing but a relentless love and pursuit in mind. Even the name Sychar was significant because it literally means "end." Jesus was traveling into enemy territory, to the end, for this moment in time. See, the Samaritan woman isn't just some random woman who makes for a good story. No! She represents the church, the bride of Christ, you and me.

Must Needs: Hebrew translation- *dei*: Behoved; necessary; needful.[2]

Jesus had already made plans to go through Samaria that day, and it was vital for Him to do so. The divine appointment with the Samaritan woman around noon in the city of Sychar at Jacob's well was necessary for Him to keep. Just as it is, right now, where you sit; it is imperative for Jesus to come to this place with you, and He made these plans. It isn't by accident that you are here. It isn't by happenstance that you are reading this right now. This is a divine appointment Jesus Christ set to meet with you.

Wow! We don't need to figure out how to get to Him; He breaks through barriers, traditional walls, religious laws, and national hindrances to get to us, to get to you, because He loves *you*.

GROUP DISCUSSION QUESTIONS

CHAPTER 1 AND CHAPTER 2

I am my beloved's, and his desire is toward me. (Song of Solomon 7:10)

You are wanted.

Beloved: darling, dear, precious, cherished, treasured, prized.

Jesus calls you His beloved and sees you right here in this moment- how does this truth make you feel?

_____

_____

_____

Desire: To want, a strong feeling of want.

What thoughts come to mind when you know Jesus desires you?

_____

_____

_____

Do you believe Jesus is the Word? Why or why not?

_____

_____

_____

What insecurities do you face when it comes to someone wanting a personal relationship with you? Be honest.

_____

_____

_____

_____

CHAPTER 3

THE ENCOUNTER

Jesus is God. He is the Son of God, but He doesn't sit on His throne, watching from afar. He didn't come to earth to die, making a way for us to get to heaven, only to leave us here to fend for ourselves. He didn't save us to turn around and leave us on our own. No! Jesus is a hands-on Savior. He is personal. He *wants you*. He wants you to *know* Him through a deep, personal, intimate relationship with Him—and not just to know *about* Him but to truly *know* Him.

Know: To perceive with certainty; to understand clearly; to have a clear and certain perception of truth, fact, or anything that actually exists.[3]

The idea of *knowing* in ancient Hebrew thought is similar to our understanding of knowing but is more personal and intimate. We may say we *know* someone but simply mean we know *about* his or her existence, but in Hebrew thought, one can *know* someone only if he or she has a personal and intimate relationship with that person. "For I know him" (Genesis 18:19). God says He knew Abraham, meaning that He had a very close relationship with Abraham. "And Adam knew Eve his wife" (Genesis 4:1), implying a very intimate relationship.

Intimate: Near; close. Close in friendship or acquaintance; familiar. One to whom the thoughts of another are entrusted without reserve.[4]

Jesus radically changed my life the moment I met Him face-to-face in Katy, Texas. I have known the story of the woman at the well all my life, but that night I had my own encounter with Jesus just as she did. I haven't been the same since. So let's open our Bibles together to John 4 and read about this amazing encounter with the Christ.

There cometh a woman of Samaria to draw water. (John 4:7)

I wonder if Jesus was smiling when the Samaritan woman approached. She was the one He had to meet, and now the moment was here. Jesus was 100 percent God and 100 percent human too. That means He experienced the same emotions we do. Was His heart racing when He saw her walking toward Him? Was His mouth suddenly dry? Did His voice crack when He first spoke to her? I know this is silly, but Jesus wasn't boring and unrelatable like most tend to paint Him. Jesus asked her to give Him something to drink. The woman responded with shock.

"Why are You even talking to me? First, I am a woman. Second, I am a Samaritan."

Jesus answered, "If thou knewest the gift of God, and Who it is that saith to thee, Give Me to drink; thou wouldest have asked of him, and he would have given thee living water." (John 4:10).

The woman replied with an obvious, logical response and questioned Jesus. How would He draw water for her? He had nothing to draw water with. Then she asked whether He was greater than Jacob, who had dug this well. Jesus answered, "Whosoever drinketh of this water shall thirst again: but whosoever drinketh of the water that I shall give him shall never thirst; but the water that I shall give him shall be in him a well of water springing up into everlasting life" (John 4:13–14).

And the woman responded with "Give me this water!"

She wanted what this living water had to offer her, a reason not to have to go to the well anymore. A reason not to have to try to avoid those who had treated her wrongfully and shamed her so much so that she had come to draw water during the hottest part of the day. But she was still missing the fact that Jesus was the Living Water. He wasn't offering her something. He was offering her Himself, a relationship with Him.

I was that woman who just wanted to have a drink of water without wanting the Giver. I wanted the provision but not the Provider. Jesus prompts our hearts and stirs them so that we will start asking ourselves, just like I did in Katy, Texas, *What am I missing? What am I lacking? What makes people want to live for You and die for You, Jesus?*

Jesus starts the conversation with us. We don't have to go to Him; He comes to us, and He speaks to us first. He begins the stirring. I sometimes wonder how many professing Christians are relying on a repeat-after-me prayer for their eternal salvation—and not on the only One who can save, Jesus. Do they just want their ticket out of hell, or do they want Him? Salvation isn't a one-and-done *thing*. It is a personal relationship with the living Savior, Jesus Christ.

Upon the request of wanting the Living Water Jesus offered, He suddenly changed the subject. At first, it looked like it was an abrupt turn, but it wasn't. He started to ask questions to expose her sin. "Go, call thy husband, and come hither" (John 4:16). She confessed she has no husband. Jesus responds with the truth that she has had five, and the one she was with now was not her husband. She'd had six men in her life, but the seventh on the scene was Jesus. Seven represents completion and perfection.

Wait, you mean to tell me I must confess my sins? The beauty of the pure, powerful living water is that it's so potent that God isn't going to give it to you for it to sit there and eventually evaporate upon your hard heart. He is going to expose your sin. He is going to reveal to you all you have done and then ask you to give it to Him. He is going to break up the hard ground and aerate the soil of your heart to bring fresh, new air into it. You can't pour water on hard, cracked ground and expect it to be absorbed. It just won't work.

Then I will sprinkle clean water upon you, and ye shall be clean: from all your filthiness, and from all your idols, will I cleanse you. A new heart also will I give you, and a new spirit will I put within you: and I will take away the stony heart out of your flesh, and I will give you an heart of flesh. And I will put my spirit within you, and cause you to walk in my statutes, and ye shall keep my judgments, and do them. (Ezekiel 36:25–27)

It isn't until the stony heart is removed that He gives you His Spirit. The Holy Spirit cannot dwell in the hardness of your heart. He must break it up, and the only way He can do that is through His prompting and exposing of your sins—and with your confession. Jesus doesn't expose your sins to shame you. It's the exact opposite. He does so because He loves you. He wants to take those things from you and give you His Spirit.

After her confession, the woman began to see that Jesus was more than just a man sitting on the side of the well. She began to tell Him the stories she had heard about the coming Messiah, who would set all things right. Even the Samaritans had heard of the coming King and that He would tell, even them, the truth of all things (John 4:25).

You have heard the stories, especially if you have gone to church your whole life or have been part of a church that has taught you the Bible. But do you know Jesus? He is seeking those who will worship Him in Spirit and in truth. Jesus isn't seeking those who worship the stories about Him or even worship the stories of what He has done in the lives of others. He is seeking those who will worship *Him*, and you can't worship Him unless you are *in* Spirit and *in* truth. Truth isn't a thing; it's not a what. It is a who, and that who is Jesus Christ.

God is a Spirit: and they that worship him must worship him in Spirit and in truth. (John 4:24)

Jesus saith unto her, I that speak unto thee am he. (John 4:26)

Think about this moment. All the stories that had been passed down through the ages, those she had heard since she was a little girl, were now being fulfilled; and she was standing before the Messiah, the Christ, the Promised One from God. She had an encounter with the Savior of the world. What a moment!

In 2003 I encountered Christ. Jesus met me right where I was, prompted questions, and exposed my sins, which brought about confession. Then with my hardened heart now broken apart before Him, He revealed to me who He was. I saw Him for the first time in my life, and I haven't been the same since. All the stories from the Bible I have known, all the stories I have heard and read about others who had an encounter with Christ, became more than stories. Jesus

became personal, real, and tangible that night. That same Jesus who met the woman at the well and met me in August 2003 is right here, in this moment.

It is necessary for Him to reveal His truth, but before He can give you His Spirit, it is also necessary for Him to expose what burdens your heart. What is it in your past or what are you currently holding so tightly to? Bitterness, anger, regret? Unforgiveness or the secrets no one else knows about? Shame and guilt? The Lord knows, and He will expose it so He can take away the stony heart and give you a heart of flesh … one that is alive! Free. Complete. Full to overflowing. Because it's His heart. All the other things that have taken His place, He wants to *expose* so He can become your one and only.

> The woman then left her waterpot, and went her way into the city, and saith to the men, Come, see a man, which told me all things that ever I did: is not this the Christ? (John 4:28)

Don't miss this! She left her waterpot, the vessel to carry water from Jacob's well, and she became the *earthen vessel*, who now carried the Living Water within her; and she ran into the town and told the people about Jesus.

> But we have this treasure in earthen vessels, that the excellency of the power may be of God, and not of us. (2 Corinthians 4:7)

> Wherefore seeing we also are compassed about with so great a cloud of witnesses, let us lay aside every weight, and the sin which doth so easily beset us, and let us run with patience the race that is set before us, looking unto Jesus the author and finisher of our faith; who for the joy that was set before him endured the cross, despising the shame, and is set down at the right hand of the throne of God. (Hebrews 12:1–2)

Jesus was the Finisher of her story. She laid aside her *weight* and all the sin that had easily beset her all her life and ran into town, like a race set before her, and she told all the men about the Man who was the Author and Finisher of her faith. He had told her all she ever did. Many of the Samaritans sought Him for themselves and came to know Jesus—not because of her testimony but because they experienced Him for themselves. They didn't encounter the woman; they encountered Jesus through her. Once the Living Water was poured into her, she splashed Him, His truth, onto every one she was around. This was the first missionary, a woman, an enemy of the Jews.

Everything we are lacking in our lives comes from Christ. He is the very essence of everything we will need, all we lack, and He is never emptied. He never runs dry. His mercies are new every morning. Great is His faithfulness. He is in full supply every single day.

> The Lord is my shepherd; I shall not want ... Thou preparest a table before me in the presence of mine enemies: thou anointest my head with oil; my cup runneth over. (Psalm 23:1, 5)

> I am the Lord thy God, which brought thee out of the land of Egypt: open thy mouth wide, and I will fill it. (Psalm 81:10)

> In the last day, that great day of the feast, Jesus stood and cried saying, If any man thirst, let him come unto me, and drink. He that believeth on me, as the scripture hath said, out of his belly shall flow rivers of living water. (John 7:37–38)

Jesus, our Bridegroom, doesn't leave us empty handed either. The groom always gives a token to the bride-to-be to seal the deal. This is a reminder that he has promised himself to her. In our culture, a man gets down on bended knee and presents the woman with a ring. Jesus stepped down out of heaven, nailed Himself to His cross, and upon our saying yes to Him, He gives us a token of promise, His seal, the Holy Spirit.

> And grieve not the holy Spirit of God, whereby ye are sealed unto the day of redemption. (Ephesians 4:30)

> For all the promises of God in him are yea, and in him Amen, unto the glory of God by us. Now he which stablisheth us with you in Christ, and hath anointed us, is God; who hath also sealed us, and given the earnest of the Spirit in our hearts. (2 Corinthians 1:20–22)

> Labour not for the meat that perisheth, but for that meat which endureth unto everlasting life, which the Son of man shall give unto you: for him hath God the Father sealed. (John 6:27)

Sealed: Fastened with a seal, confirmed, closed.[5]

> The works of his hands are verity and judgment; all his commandments are sure. They stand fast for ever and ever, and are done in truth and uprightness. He sent redemption unto his people: he hath commanded his covenant for ever: holy and reverend is his name. (Psalm 111:7–9)

Covenant: A mutual consent or agreement of two or more persons; to do or to forbear some act or thing. A contract; stipulation. A covenant is created by deed *in writing*, sealed and executed; or it may be implied in the contract; the promises of God.[6]

Sealed. Covenant. Betrothed. We are His. What a Savior!

Who is He to you? Do you know the stories about Him? Do you know how He changed those around you? But what has He done for you? What is your encounter with Jesus? I promise you that if you have had an encounter with Him, you will know it, because you can't help but share it. When you know Him personally, when you experience the Christ, all you want to do is worship and praise Him. All you want to do is talk about Him and spend time with Him.

If you have a personal relationship with Jesus, then the next question to consider is this. What do you value the most in your relationship with Jesus? Please hear me. Don't just throw out the answer you think you are supposed to say, because we have all done it. Be honest with yourself for a minute and take time to analyze what you value the most with Jesus. Is it what He can give or do for you that is valued the most? Or is Jesus whom you hold most precious?

God showed me something new to answer these questions in the story of Moses. Take a minute, turn to Deuteronomy, and read chapters 31–34. Ask the Lord to show you something new from this all-familiar story.

I have always put emphasis on what Moses missed out on in these passages. Moses wasn't able to cross into the Promised Land after wandering in the wilderness for forty years because of his disobedience by striking the rock (Numbers 20). I think I have heard more sermons on that part of the story than anything else, but look with me at what the Lord opened my eyes to.

> And Moses went up from the plains of Moab unto the mountain of Nebo, to the top of Pisgah, that is over against Jericho. And the Lord shewed him all the land of Gilead, unto Dan … And the Lord said unto him, This is the land which I sware unto Abraham, unto Isaac, and unto Jacob, saying, I will give it unto thy seed: I have caused thee to see it with thine eyes, but thou shalt not go over thither. So Moses the servant of the Lord died there in the land of Moab, according to the word of the Lord. (Deuteronomy 34:1, 4–5)

Although Moses was able to see the Promised Land, he wasn't able to place his feet on that promise given to God's people; this whole time I have felt bad for Moses. I hope I'm not the only one who has had this thought. But here is the truth. Moses was able to experience something far greater. Do you want to guess what that is? Moses saw the face of God!

And there arose not a prophet since in Israel like unto Moses, whom the Lord knew face to face. (Deuteronomy 34:10)

This story began to raise numerous questions in my heart. What do I want more? Do I want the promise? Or the Promise Maker? Do I want the healing or the Healer? Do I want heaven or Him?

> Not every one that saith unto me, Lord, Lord, shall enter into the kingdom of heaven; but he that doeth the will of my Father which is in heaven. Many will say to me in that day, Lord, Lord, have we not prophesied in thy name? and in thy name have cast out devils? and in thy name done many wonderful works? And then I will profess unto them, I never knew you: depart from me, ye that work iniquity. (Matthew 7:21–23)

Have you ever been real, raw, and vulnerable before Him? Allowing Him to expose all the junk in your life? Have you ever confessed those things to receive the Living Water that transforms you and your life? If that has never happened, then, precious one, may I lovingly ask, have you ever truly been born again? It's not a prayer that saves; it's Jesus. It's not the ministry work and the good, moral things that save; it is the Christ. It would be a travesty if you knew Jesus was waiting for you at the well but completely ignored Him. Or if He stirred your heart, prompting questions to expose what was beneath the hardness of your heart, having a small conversation with Him, but you weren't truthful with Him. Maybe you chose to hide what was buried in the soil or became angry and justified why you are the way you are and blamed it on others and situations.

You have two options. First is to walk away and miss Jesus. Miss the encounter with Christ. Miss the uncomfortable and painful exposure of sin that opens your eyes to truly see Him for who He is. Miss eternal life with Him and an abundant life in Him while on this earth. Or you can embrace the stirring of the Holy Spirit and the exposure of sin. Confess it, whatever it may be, and give it to Him. Then allow Him to give you Himself … the Living Water.

The encounter the woman at the well had with Jesus wasn't only for her. It is for every one of us. No matter what you have done, no matter what others say about you, no matter what life has handed down to you—it doesn't matter. Jesus came. He is here with you, and He desires to have a relationship with you, take away the weight of sin you carry, and give you Himself. Do you *know* Him?

IF YOU KNEW

BY ANGELA MORGAN

If you knew my Jesus,

You would know the Champion of your soul.

You would know that He sticks closer than anyone will.

You would know that He will never leave or forsake you.

You would know that His very Word washes away all the lies spoken over you.

You would know that He gives joy in the midst of suffering.

You would know that He gives peace in the midst of chaos.

You would know that He fights your battles if you let Him.

You would know that He feeds you when you are hungry.

You would know that He gives you drink when you are thirsty.

You would know He prays for you.

You would know that in this life it is worth it all to know Him and be known by Him.

You would know that He has saved you and secured your eternal destiny.

You would know that *one* day you will get to see Him face-to-face.

You would know that Jesus is worth it all.

GROUP DISCUSSION QUESTIONS

CHAPTER 3: THE ENCOUNTER

Jesus answered and said unto her, If thou knewest the gift of God, and who it is that saith to thee, Give me to drink; thou wouldest have asked of him, and he would have given thee living water.

(John 4:10)

Do you believe that Jesus wants you? Why or why not?

_____

_____

_____

_____

_____

_____

What do you think having "abundant life" means?

_____

_____

_____

_____

_____

_____

How do you respond to the truth that Jesus "must needs" come to where you are? What other verses can you find that show Jesus comes to us?

_____

_____

_____

_____

_____

_____

Have you come to the place in your life that you know and live in the freedom that the sins of your past are forgiven and gone? If so, what are some of the scriptures the Lord has used to give you confidence in this truth?

_____

_____

_____

_____

_____

_____

Who is Jesus to you? (Be honest.)

_____

_____

_____

_____

_____

_____

CHAPTER 4

THE TEMPLE

(Tabernacle, House, Sanctuary)

I honestly believe the foundation of this study is to know who we are and whose we are. A good place to start this journey of discovery is with God's temple.

> What? know ye not that your body is the temple of the Holy Ghost which is in you, which ye have of God, and ye are not your own? For ye are bought with a price: therefore glorify God in your body, and in your spirit, which are God's. (1 Corinthians 6:19–20)

I am amazed that of all topics and stories in the Bible, there are none more detailed in written form than those about the tabernacle or temple. Scripture lists detail after detail about how it would be built, the materials used to build it, who would build it, what tools would be used, the order of the assembling, what the priests would do, and even what they would wear. The list goes on and on from Exodus 25 to Exodus 40.

It's safe to say that God is serious about His temple.

Exodus:

25:1–9	The materials for the sanctuary
25:10–22	The ark of the covenant
25:23–30	The table of the bread of presence
25:31–40	The lampstand
26:1–36	The tabernacle's ten curtains, the veil, and its colors: blue, scarlet, and purple
27:1–8	The altar
27:9–19	The courtyard
27:20–21	Offering the oil
28: 1–43	The clothing of the priests
29:1–46	The consecration of Aaron and his sons
30:1–10	The altar of incense
30:11–16	The ransom money
30:17–21	The bronze laver
30:22–38	Oil and Incense

Question:

If God is that serious about the Old Testament temple, how much more serious is He about the temple He sent His Son, Jesus Christ, to die for?

If you are a child of God, you are His temple. For us to appreciate the relationship we have with God, we must grasp the depth and magnitude of that truth to know and understand the intensity of what was done for us.

> But Christ as a son over his own house; whose house are we, if we hold fast the confidence and the rejoicing of the hope firm unto the end. (Hebrews 3:6)

> What? know ye not that your body is the temple of the Holy Ghost. (1 Corinthians 6:19)

If you are born again, Jesus bought you. He bought your body and made it His temple. The Lord didn't just place details on what the doors, curtains, and panels would look like that would

make up the outside of the tabernacle, but the items or furniture to be placed in the temple were of a greater significance than what was seen on the outside. These items were placed in a specific divine order that is *still* significant and applicable to us today. Check it out:

THE ALTAR

The altar of sacrifice was a place where sin was atoned for. Sin must be dealt with and confessed before I can receive anything from God. ("Go, call thy husband" … "I have no husband" [John 4:16–17].)

THE LAVER OF WASHING

The laver was a vessel for washing, a large basin; in scripture history, it was a basin placed in the court of the Jewish tabernacle, where the priests washed their hands and feet.

This represents the Living Water. It is only after we have been washed and made new and clean that the Holy Spirit can now dwell within.

THE GOLDEN LAMPSTAND

In the tabernacle, the lampstand was to be placed in the first section, called the "holy place." It was to give forth light day and night, and was the only source of light. The lampstand as a whole was to be in the shape of a tree with the base and center part representing the trunk with three "branches" on each side. The top of each branch was to be made like an open almond flower, and each flower held an oil lamp. The most important thing to note about the lampstand is that it points to Christ, as do *all* the elements of the tabernacle.

For those who have been born again, that Light, Jesus (John 1:1–9), now dwells in us, and we can now have fellowship with the Light when we choose to walk in the Light (1 John 1:7). And because we are in His light, in His presence, we can partake of the next piece of furniture.

THE SHEWBREAD

These are loaves of bread the priest placed before the Lord on the golden table in the sanctuary. They were shaped like a brick, were ten palms long and five wide, and weighed about eight pounds each. They were made of fine flour, unleavened, and changed every sabbath. The loaves were twelve in number and represented the twelve tribes of Israel. Only the priests were allowed to eat them.

The shewbread was a representation of the Bread of Life, the Word of God, Jesus (Jeremiah 15:16).

THE ALTAR OF INCENSE

This can be seen as a picture of the prayers of God's people. Our prayers ascend to God as the smoke of the incense ascended in the sanctuary. As the incense was burned with fire from the altar of burnt offering, our prayers must be kindled with heaven's grace. The fact that the incense was always burning means we should always pray. The altar of incense was holy to the Lord and was atoned for with the blood of the sacrifice; it is *only* the blood of Christ applied to our hearts that makes our prayers acceptable. Our prayers are holy because of Jesus's sacrifice; therefore, they are pleasing to God.

We have confessed at the altar and were washed by the Word at the laver of washing. Now that we are clean, we have access to the holy place, where the Light illuminates His Word for nourishment so we can offer up prayer from His Word.

THE MERCY SEAT

The Greek word for mercy seat in Hebrews 9:5 is *hilasterion*, which basically means propitiation. It carries the idea of the removal of sin. Christ is now our propitiation. He became sin for us. The sacrifice of Jesus is also a continuous reminder that the veil has been torn and that we can now run boldly to God's very presence. Why? Because the blood of Jesus was once applied for my sins and yours. We no longer need to sprinkle the blood of goats and lambs over the mercy seat. Jesus paid it all. His blood has been applied to my life.

I believe that every intricate detail laid out in Exodus about the tabernacle is intended to show two important things. First, God is in the details. Details are important to Him, and He is serious about how things are made, what is inside them, and what their function is. Second, God is just as serious about the details of you and me: what we allow in our hearts, minds, and bodies; and what we do with what He has given us. Some of the details are ones we don't really think about. Let's look at some together.

Jesus thinks of you so much that if you were to count the number of His thoughts toward you, they would be more than the sands of the sea.

> How precious also are thy thoughts unto me, O God! how great is the sum of them! If I should count them, they are more in number than the sand: when I awake, I am still with thee. (Psalm 139:17–18)

Jesus keeps all your tears in a bottle.

Thou tellest my wanderings: put thou my tears into thy bottle: are they not in thy book? (Psalm 56:8)

Your prayers are in a golden vial in heaven, and it fills the throne room with its sweet aroma.

And when he had taken the book, the four beasts and four and twenty elders fell down before the Lamb, having every one of them harps, and golden vials full of odours, which are the prayers of saints. (Revelation 5:8)

Jesus counts your steps.

Doth not he see my ways, and count all my steps? (Job 31:4)

He has your name engraved on the palm of His hands.

Behold, I have graven thee upon the palms of my hands; thy walls are continually before me. (Isaiah 49:16)

He has numbered the hairs on your head.

But the very hairs of your head are all numbered. (Matthew 10:30)

He died for you and paid your penalty so you would never be separated from Him ever again.

For God so loved the world, that he gave his only begotten Son, that whosoever believeth in him should not perish, but have everlasting life. (John 3:16)

I would say He is serious about us. He knows everything and wants everything, all of us. He bought everything, knowing what we were—enemies of the truth; selfish, wicked sinners. Yet He purchased us by the precious blood of the Lamb to give us new life in Him. It's not just our life anymore. Yes, we still have a free will, and yes, Jesus won't force us to choose Him, but if only we knew the One who loves us and wants us to be found in Him. If we only knew what took place for us to be His. The only way for us to know that is by being in the Word every single day.

Jesus values you. If you have accepted Christ as your personal Savior, He resides in you, and every detail about you and your life matters to Him.

The order of the elements in the Old Testament tabernacle is parallel to the order of the New Testament temple, which is *you*. The truths in this *Wanted* study won't take root until we understand and appreciate what being the temple of the Holy Spirit of God means and the cost Jesus paid to redeem us to Himself.

GROUP DISCUSSION QUESTIONS

CHAPTER 4: THE TEMPLE

What? know ye not that your body is the temple of the Holy Ghost which is in you, which ye have of God, and ye are not your own? For ye are bought with a price: therefore glorify God in your body, and in your spirit, which are God's. (1 Corinthians 6:19–20)

What thoughts come to mind as you come to understand you are *now* the temple of the Holy Spirit? What other scriptures come to mind when you think about this truth?

_____

_____

_____

_____

_____

_____

How do you feel after seeing how detailed the first tabernacle was and knowing God is just as much, if not more, detailed about you, the *temple* He sent His Son to die for?

_____

_____

_____

_____

_____

What about your Temple are you most concerned with? The outer appearance that everyone sees or what's within that only Jesus sees? Be honest.

_____

_____

_____

_____

Do you desire to beautify the temple of your life or body? If so, what are some things you need to remove from your life? What are some things you need to add?

_____

_____

_____

_____

_____

_____

What are your thoughts after understanding the price that was paid for you to be called the temple of the Holy Spirit?

_____

_____

_____

_____

_____

_____

CHAPTER 5

WANTED

W: WATER

W: WATER

Jesus wants to *water* you.

He is your Living Water.

> For I have satiated the weary soul, and I have replenished every sorrowful soul. (Jeremiah 31:25)

Satiate: To fill, to satisfy an appetite or desire. To furnish, to fill beyond natural desire, desire to the utmost.[7]

We were all born with an appetite. We are always looking for something to fill that desire and satisfy us. But as we grow up, we don't go to the only One who can supply. We go to everything and everyone else, which leaves us lacking. We feel unwanted because the desire within us isn't being fulfilled. We don't realize in that moment that the longing we have within us is meant only for the One, Jesus Christ.

> They shall be abundantly satisfied with the fatness of thy house; and thou shalt make them drink of the river of thy pleasures. (Psalm 36:8)

> Thou wilt shew me the path of life: in thy presence is fullness of joy; at thy right hand there are pleasures for evermore. (Psalm 16:11)

When the Bible talks about having pleasures, it means being filled with happiness, delight, joy and contentment. Being completely satisfied when we drink of the rivers of the Lord's pleasures. We just talked about our bodies being the temples of God. In Psalm 36, the Word says we "shall be abundantly satisfied"—not "might be" but "shall be." Friend, that's a promise. What will satisfy us? The river of God's pleasures. Our God isn't a boring God. He wants to pour into us every single day.

I Am the Woman at the Well

Let's take a moment and remember our first encounter with the Christ (John 4).

Jesus "must needs go through Samaria" (vv. 1–5). Jesus knew the woman would be there (vv. 6–7).

Describe your first encounter with Jesus. Where were you?

_____

_____

_____

_____

_____

Jesus asked her to give Him a drink (v. 7). What did He say or ask that prompted you to inquire more of Him?

_____

_____

_____

_____

_____

The woman was shocked that He was talking to her, a woman of Samaria (v. 9).

What doubts or insecurities did you have?

_____

_____

_____

_____

Jesus presented her with Living Water (v. 10). Do you remember the date or month and year when Jesus presented you with this precious gift from God?

_____

_____

_____

_____
_____

The woman asked for the Living Water (v. 15).

Has there been a true change *within* you? Or was it just an outward *appearance* of a changed life?

_____
_____
_____
_____
_____

Jesus changed the subject and told her to call her husband (v. 16).

`Aerate: To expose to the air, to break up.`

You cannot pour water onto hard, cracked ground and expect it to soak in. The water will only rest on top and eventually evaporate. You must break up the ground and expose it to the air. It must be brought to light for it to become healthy enough to have new life and new growth. Which is why Jesus brought up her husband—not in a condemning tone or attitude but to prompt a confession, an unmasking of where she was turning to fill a deep longing within her. He desired to break up the dried, parched soil of her hardened heart, so when He revealed who He was, her heart could receive Him, the Living Water.

What was the sin Jesus exposed in your life?

_____
_____
_____
_____
_____

The woman responded with truth. "I have no husband" (v. 17).

Did you confess what Jesus exposed? Did you release those things and give them to Him?

_____
_____
_____

_____

_____

The woman said, "I know that Messias cometh which is called Christ" (v. 25).

Are you basing your salvation on the stories you know and have heard or a repeat-after-me prayer?

_____

_____

_____

_____

_____

Jesus revealed to her who He was, the Christ (v. 26). Explain the moment you saw Jesus for who He is.

_____

_____

_____

_____

_____

The woman immediately responded by telling others about Him (vv. 28–29). How did you respond after you met Christ?

_____

_____

_____

_____

_____

It's good to remember that we encountered Christ at the well that one time, but He is also the supply we need every single day. If we don't go to Him, spending time with Him and abiding in the Living Water, we will become hard, cracked, and calloused again. We will seek other pleasures and things to fill our lives, just like we did before; and those things will leave us empty, annoyed, frustrated, and depressed all over again.

There is a constant battle between the flesh and the Spirit, and we choose which we will abide in. The Living Water has remedies within it that washes away not only the sin in our lives but also the cravings and longings for those sins that come daily. It's like a river or stream that constantly moves, washing away rocks and sand, exposing what is beneath. As long as we are in this world, we need to be in that constant flowing river of the Living Water so He can wash away and expose the things that need to be removed from our lives, ushering in clarity and new life.

> Then washed I thee with water; yea, I throughly washed away thy blood from thee, and I anointed thee with oil. (Ezekiel 16:9)

> Now the God of hope fill you with all joy and peace in believing, that ye may abound in hope, through the power of the Holy Ghost. (Romans 15:13)

Abound: To be in great plenty of, great quantity of.[8]

> The thief cometh not, but for to steal, and to kill, and to destroy: I am come that they might have life, and that they might have it more abundantly. (John 10:10)

I don't know about you, but I'm tired of living the *less-than* life. I want the abundant life! I want to live in the fulfillment He has for me to live. He is everything I have ever needed, and I want to experience all that. Don't you? And that's what Romans 15:13 says. He wants to fill us. Our source for having the abundant life is the Living Water, Jesus Christ.

> And such were some of you: but ye are washed, but ye are sanctified, but ye are justified in the name of the Lord Jesus, and by the Spirit of our God. (1 Corinthians 6:11)

> In the last day, that great day of the feast, Jesus stood and cried saying, If any man thirst, let him come unto me, and drink. He that believeth on me, as the scripture hath said, out of his belly shall flow rivers of living water. (John 7:37–38)

What you allow to be poured into you will be what comes out of you. That's just the truth. If I fill myself with good things in my life, then good things will come out of my life. Jesus is what is good. Time with Jesus is an investment—not just for me but for everyone around me.

> I call heaven and earth to record this day against you, that I have set before you life and death, blessing and cursing: therefore choose life, that both thou and thy seed may live: That thou mayest love the Lord thy God, and that thou mayest obey his voice, and that thou mayest cleave unto him: for he is thy life, and the length of thy days. (Deuteronomy 30:19–20)

Choice: The voluntary act of selecting or separating from two or more things that which is preferred; or the determination of the mind in preferring one thing to another; election.[9]

We live in a world that has a hard time taking responsibility for the choices and actions we have made. I know we do because I'm guilty of doing so myself. We blame it on how we were raised or on our DNA, chemical imbalances, or being a product of circumstances we aren't responsible for. So we tend to express this with outbursts of negative emotions that come billowing out of our mouths. This same mindset sadly has our culture bound and chained to depression and lies of the enemy. What you allow to be poured into your life will be what you think daily. What you think will eventually lead to how you act and the choices you make.

Whatever we think in our hearts is who we are (Proverbs 27:3), and, precious one, you are in control of that. Not your circumstances, those around you, or your health. You are. Just like Joshua proclaimed that he would choose that day and every day to serve the Lord (Joshua 24:15), it is also our choice whom we will serve. Proverbs 4:20–27 shows us how we serve the Lord. It is by getting in the Word. We *attend* to the Word. We don't let it depart from us. We keep it in the midst of our hearts. Attending to the Word means choosing to read and study the Word rather than choosing TV. Listening to the Word means going to seek wisdom and guidance from the Word, not from social media. It means even choosing to spend time in prayer and the Word instead of choosing to hang out with friends. Memorize the Word instead of the lyrics to the latest hit song. When we direct our attention to the Word of God, allowing the Living Water to be what is poured into us, our thoughts align with God, and then so do our actions. Whatever goes in must come out.

> So shall my word be that goeth forth out of my mouth: it shall not return unto me void, but it shall accomplish that which I please, and it shall prosper in the thing whereto I sent it. (Isaiah 55:11)

The Word, Jesus, doesn't return void in our lives. He goes out and accomplishes everything He said He would do. He not only accomplishes it, but the Bible says it will prosper. It will continue and not die. These bodies will die, but the Word within us will be passed on from generation to generation until the Lord Jesus comes back.

Wow! What a promise! The vision, the calling, Jesus has given to all mankind never dies, and we are invited to be part of His purpose, to be on mission with Him. He doesn't need us to do anything, but He wants us. He desires a personal relationship with us and wants us to be part of what He is doing. Not just here in this day and time, but he wants us to be part of the whole thing. That is the whole point of being filled with the Holy Spirit.

…but be filled with the Spirit. (Ephesians 5:18)

But the fruit of the Spirit is love, joy, peace, longsuffering, gentleness, goodness, faith, meekness, temperance: against such there is no law. (Galatians 5:22–23)

If we are filled with the Holy Spirit and allowing the Living Water to pour into us every day, then the fruit of the Spirit will be evident in how we live our lives. What are you pouring out? The world is in desperate need of Jesus, but they won't be able to encounter Him if we aren't being filled daily by Him through His Word. It will be like trying to draw water from a dry well.

Speaking to yourselves in psalms and hymns and spiritual songs, singing and making melody in your heart to the Lord. (Ephesians 5:19)

Speaking to yourselves means pouring out. It is pouring out onto one another the hope of Jesus, the truth of Jesus, and the love of Jesus. We should be encouraging one another in and through the Word. It can be through reading and sharing scripture, singing together, or praying. We should edify and lift each other up in and by the Word.

What are you putting into His temple? TV, Netflix, social media, corrupt communication, gossip, and music that doesn't glorify Him? If I'm bought with a price, if I'm now filled with the Holy Spirit, don't you think the things that come out of me should be God things? Shouldn't they be words and actions that are constantly edifying and encouraging the body of Christ? All things by Him, through Him, to Him, and for His glory! That is what should be coming out of our lives. They should abound from us!

And to know the love of Christ, which passeth knowledge, that ye might be filled with all the fullness of God. (Ephesians 3:19)

So that the priests could not stand to minister by reason of the cloud: for the glory of the Lord had filled the house of God. (2 Chronicles 5:14)

But whosoever drinketh of the water that I shall give him shall never thirst; but the water that I shall give him shall be in him a well of water springing up into everlasting life. (John 4:14)

I should let the Word of Christ come out of me like a geyser that splashes onto everyone around me. Jesus should be rushing out of our talk and walk like rivers of water, but we cannot do that if we aren't connected to or abiding *in* the source, the Living Water. The only way to do that is to make spending personal time with our Savior a priority. We must value Him above every other relationship or thing. He is what is needful, not my ideas, thoughts, suggestions, logic, understanding, and so on. It's Jesus. Just Jesus. He is the source of life and life abundantly.

He has allowed us to tap into His Living Water to give us life. He has allowed us to be a vessel to be poured into so we can pour out His Living Water onto all those around us. We are filled to pour out.

> Blessed be God, even the Father of our Lord Jesus Christ, the Father of mercies, and the God of all comfort; who comforteth us in all our tribulation, that we may be able to comfort them which are in any trouble, by the comfort wherewith we ourselves are comforted of God. (2 Corinthians 1:3–4)

How do we let Him love and fill us? It is by praying and seeking His face. We seek His face by getting in the Word. I am a visual learner. One day the Lord showed me what this looks like. He had me hold an empty cup under the faucet and turn on the water. I watched the water fill the cup, spill over onto my hand, and splash on everything around the cup. As long as the cup stayed under the steady stream of water, the water continued to overflow from within it, splashing, and covering everything around it with water. It wasn't the cup that was covering my hand; it wasn't the cup that was splashing onto the other dishes in the sink. It was the water!

We are the cups. We are the vessels Jesus fills to overflowing so He, not us, can affect those around us, so others can experience Him through us. That is the whole point. But again, we cannot do that unless we choose to remain under the Source. We choose whether we allow the Holy Spirit to flow in and out of us or whether we quench Him.

> My beloved is mine, and I am his. (Song of Solomon 2:16)

> I am my beloved's, and his desire is toward me. (Song of Solomon 7:10)

> When thou saidst, Seek ye my face; my heart said unto thee, Thy face, Lord, will I seek. (Psalm 27:8)

The Living Water wants to water us. It's His character. It's His nature. It's the very essence of who He is. He is a Giver. He loves to give us everything He has. It all goes back to the intimate relationship with Him. Jesus is serious about you. He loves you. He bought you.

> Jesus answered and said unto her, If thou knewest the gift of God, and who it is that saith to thee, Give me to drink; thou wouldest have asked of him, and he would have given thee living water. (John 4:10)

Lord Jesus, thank You. Thank You for coming to where I am and meeting with me. Thank You for breaking up the hard ground of my heart so that I can receive truth, so I can receive

You! Thank You for Your willingness to pour into me Living Water that will never run dry. Thank You for satisfying my dry, thirsty soul and satiating my parched heart. Your love and desire towards me leave me overwhelmed and in awe of You. Thank You for loving me, pursuing me, and wanting me. I love You, Lord. In Jesus's name.

Beloved, you are wanted.

You are watered.

GROUP DISCUSSION QUESTIONS

CHAPTER 5

W: Water

For I have satiated the weary soul, and I have replenished every sorrowful soul. (Jeremiah 31:25)

In Psalm 36:8, the Word says we "shall be" abundantly satisfied by the rivers of God's pleasures. What do you think that means? What are some other verses that say the Lord will satisfy you?

_____

_____

_____

_____

_____

Now the God of hope fill you with all joy and peace in believing, that ye may abound in hope, through the power of the Holy Ghost. (Romans 15:13)

Do you live in the fullness of Romans 15:13? Why or why not?

_____

_____

_____

_____

_____

What we pour into our lives will be what pours out from us daily. What are you allowing to be poured into your life the most?

_____

_____

_____

_____

_____

What areas of your heart need to be aerated by the Word to soften it to receive the gift of Living Water? What things are blocking you from living the abundant life?

_____

_____

_____

_____

_____

CHAPTER 6

wANTED

A: ADORN

A: ADORN

Jesus wants to *adorn* you.

Jesus is our robe of righteousness.

`Adorn: To make more beautiful, enhance, beautify.`

> Blessed be the Lord God of our fathers, which hath put such a thing as this in the king's heart, to beautify the house of the Lord which is in Jerusalem. (Ezra 7:27)

The synonym of *adorn* is grace. It is because of His grace and His death that we can be adorned by His robe of righteousness. It is His robe that He freely gives to us.

> For if by one man's offence death reigned by one; much more they which receive abundance of grace and of the gift of righteousness shall reign in life by one, Jesus Christ. Therefore as by the offence of one judgment came upon all men to condemnation; even so by the righteousness of one the free gift came upon all men unto justification of life. For as by one man's disobedience many were made sinners, so by the obedience of one shall many be made righteous. (Romans 5:17–19)

It is by His grace that we are redeemed and offered this freedom garment. Friend, if you have never called on the name of Jesus to save you, I urge you, please do not wait. He was stripped of everything so you may have everything. He lovingly took your place, battled your enemy, and rose in victory so you never have to experience hell and separation from Him. He loves *you*. He wants *you*.

> And they crucified him, and parted his garments, casting lots: that it might be fulfilled which was spoken by the prophet, They parted my garments among them, and upon my vesture did they cast lots. (Matthew 27:35)

Jesus was stripped naked so we could be clothed, not with just any garment but with His garment. Not just with any robe but His robe.

> Go ye therefore into the highways, and as many as ye shall find, bid to the marriage. So those servants went out into the highways, and gathered together all as many as they found, both bad and good: and the wedding was furnished with guests. And when the king came in to see the guests, he saw there a man

which had not on a wedding garment: And he saith unto him, Friend, how camest thou in hither not having a wedding garment? And he was speechless. Then said the king to the servants, Bind him hand and foot, and take him away, and cast him into outer darkness; there shall be weeping and gnashing of teeth. (Matthew 22:9–13)

The only way to be in His presence and be in heaven with Him for all eternity is to have the wedding garment. What is this wedding garment? What does this mean?

If so be that ye have heard him, and have been taught by him, as the truth is in Jesus: That ye put off concerning the former conversation the old man, which is corrupt according to the deceitful lusts; And be renewed in the spirit of your mind; And that ye put on the new man, which after God is created in righteousness and true holiness. (Ephesians 4:21–24)

And the son said unto him, Father, I have sinned against heaven, and in thy sight, and am no more worthy to be called thy son. But the father said to his servants, Bring forth the best robe, and put it on him; and put a ring on his hand, and shoes on his feet. (Luke 15:21–22)

Sometimes we forget that the robe is His best one, that the Father's best is Jesus, and it's a one size fits all.

For God so loved the world, that he gave his only begotten Son, that whosoever believeth in him should not perish, but have everlasting life. (John 3:16)

I will greatly rejoice in the Lord, my soul shall be joyful in my God; for he hath clothed me with the garments of salvation, he hath covered me with the robe of righteousness, as a bridegroom decketh himself with ornaments, and as a bride adorneth herself with her jewels. (Isaiah 61:10)

Righteous: Blameless, innocent, justified.

Understand that when God places His robe of righteousness on you, He sees only the robe you are covered with. He sees only Jesus, and that means you are blameless in His sight.

One of the best explanations of the word *justified* is just as if I never sinned.

I thank my God always on your behalf, for the grace of God which is given you by Jesus Christ; that in every thing ye are enriched by him, in all utterance, and in all knowledge; even as the testimony of Christ was confirmed in you: so that

ye come behind in no gift; waiting for the coming of our Lord Jesus Christ: who shall also confirm you unto the end, that ye may be blameless in the day of our Lord Jesus Christ. God is faithful, by whom ye were called unto the fellowship of his Son Jesus Christ our Lord. (1 Corinthians 1:4–9)

We are enriched by Him; to be enriched means to bring fullness to. Do you remember who fills us? As we get to know Him, He will bring fullness to our lives. We won't lack anything. We will be spiritually wealthy children of the King, and that, dear one, is a life of abundance Jesus came to give us. Everything that amounts to any value, holiness, and righteousness has nothing to do with us but everything to do with Him. Who clothed you? The Father. What did He clothe you with? His Son, Jesus Christ.

> I clothed thee also with broidered work, and shod thee with badgers' skin, and I girded thee about with fine linen, and I covered thee with silk. I decked thee also with ornaments, and I put bracelets upon thy hands, and a chain on thy neck. And I put a jewel on thy forehead, and earrings in thine ears, and a beautiful crown upon thine head. Thus wast thou decked with gold and silver; and thy raiment was of fine linen, and silk, and broidered work; thou didst eat fine flour, and honey, and oil: and thou wast exceeding beautiful, and thou didst prosper into a kingdom. And thy renown went forth among the heathen for thy beauty: for it was perfect through my comeliness, which I had put upon thee, saith the Lord God. (Ezekiel 16:10–14)

Comeliness: That which is becoming, fit, or suitable in form or manner. Comeliness of a person implies symmetry or due proportion of parts.[10]

What a beautiful picture of how Christ adorns us with Himself! It is His beauty the world sees, and He makes us beautiful. It isn't through the things of the world or what we do. It is Jesus. He will beautify you through His comeliness. His beauty is what makes us beautiful.

In a Galilean wedding, once the proposal is made, the bridegroom goes away and begins to prepare a house for his bride, and the bride immediately begins to prepare herself for the wedding, for her bridegroom. Neither she nor the bridegroom knows the day when he will come to get her; only the father knows the day. In light of that fact, spiritually speaking, how do we beautify ourselves, His temple, to prepare for our soon-coming Bridegroom? It is through prayer and the Word. It is through spending time with Him every single day.

He greatly desires your beauty.

I am my beloved's, and his desire is toward me. (Song of Solomon 7:10)

He desires you. He wants you. In fact, it's such a burning want that it sent Him to the cross to die for you.

When we get to that place where we desire Him as much as He desires us, when we are passionately in love with the Savior, when we want and are willing to put to death the carnal things of our flesh that rob us from the time we get to spend with Him and take our focus off Him, that's when we start to beautify the house. He desires that! He wants that time with us.

We need to remind ourselves of what took place for us to receive the robe of righteousness. There is a trade that happens when you become a daughter of the King of kings and Lord of lords. What was the trade? Jesus became (took on Himself) sin for us so we might be made the righteousness of God in Him. Christ takes our sins, and we take His righteousness.

> Christ hath redeemed us from the curse of the law, being made a curse for us:
> for it is written, Cursed is every one that hangeth on a tree: that the blessing
> of Abraham might come on the Gentiles through Jesus Christ; that we might
> receive the promise of the Spirit through faith. (Galatians 3:13–14)

What was physically seen by those who were there through the beatings, scourging, mocking, and crucifixion of Jesus Christ do not even come close to the truth of what all He had to endure. In this generation, we may watch movies and read books on the graphic descriptions of it, but again, it doesn't even begin to shed light on the reality of what Jesus experienced. It wasn't just the physical things Jesus went through, but it was a spiritual battle against Satan, sin, death, hell, and the grave. It was the taking on of God's wrath. It was the separation from God, the Father.

This is the trade God made for us:

- Jesus took our sins. We take His righteousness.
- Jesus took the suffering. We get to go free.
- Jesus was stripped naked. We are clothed.
- Jesus was put to death. We are born again.
- Jesus became a curse. We are blessed.

THE BLESSING

Blessed: To enjoy spiritual happiness and having favor with God.[11]

You are God's favorite because Jesus Christ is in you and *on* you. We get to have all the meaning of the blessing and receive them as well because Jesus chose to become a curse to God. His choice allows us to experience eternal and physical blessing of health, friendships, and eternal rewards.

As you read the next portion of scripture, circle every time you see the words *blessed*, *blessing*, or *bless*.

> And all these blessings shall come on thee, and overtake thee, if thou shalt hearken unto the voice of the Lord thy God. Blessed shalt thou be in the city, and blessed shalt thou be in the field. Blessed shall be the fruit of thy body, and the fruit of thy ground, and the fruit of thy cattle, the increase of thy kine, and the flocks of thy sheep. Blessed shall be thy basket and thy store. Blessed shalt thou be when thou comest in, and blessed shalt thou be when thou goest out. The Lord shall cause thine enemies that rise up against thee to be smitten before thy face: they shall come out against thee one way, and flee before thee seven ways. The Lord shall command the blessing upon thee in thy storehouses, and in all that thou settest thine hand unto; and he shall bless thee in the land which the Lord thy God giveth thee. The Lord shall establish thee an holy people unto himself, as he hath sworn unto thee, if thou shalt keep the commandments of the Lord thy God, and walk in his ways. And all people of the earth shall see that thou art called by the name of the Lord; and they shall be afraid of thee. And the Lord shall make thee plenteous in goods, in the fruit of thy body, and in the fruit of thy cattle, and in the fruit of thy ground, in the land which the Lord sware unto thy fathers to give thee. The Lord shall open unto thee his good treasure, the heaven to give the rain unto thy land in his season, and to bless all the work of thine hand: and thou shalt lend unto many nations, and thou shalt not borrow. And the Lord shall make thee the head, and not the tail; and thou shalt be above only, and thou shalt not be beneath; if that thou hearken unto the commandments of the Lord thy God, which I command thee this day, to observe and to do them: And thou shalt not go aside from any of the words which I command thee this day, to the right hand, or to the left, to go after other gods to serve them. (Deuteronomy 28:2–14)

THE CURSE

Cursed: Affliction, torment, great vexation; condemned; absolute misery; detestable. Detestable means disgusted, repulsive, or offensive.[12]

It's hard for me to say these words about my Savior, but Jesus became disgusting, repulsive, and detestable for us. He became cursed so we could become a blessing. Wow.

Again, as you read the following, circle every time you see the word *cursed*, *curse*, *destroyed*, *vexed*, or anything related to being cursed.

> But it shall come to pass, if thou wilt not hearken unto the voice of the Lord thy God, to observe to do all his commandments and his statutes which I command thee this day; that all these curses shall come upon thee, and overtake thee: Cursed shalt thou be in the city, and cursed shalt thou be in the field. Cursed shall be thy basket and thy store. Cursed shall be the fruit of thy body, and the fruit of thy land, the increase of thy kin*e*, and the flocks of thy sheep. Cursed shalt thou be when thou comest in, and cursed shalt thou be when thou goest out. The Lord shall send upon thee cursing, vexation, and rebuke, in all that thou settest thine hand unto for to do, until thou be destroyed, and until thou perish quickly; because of the wickedness of thy doings, whereby thou hast forsaken me. The Lord shall make the pestilence cleave unto thee, until he have consumed thee from off the land, whither thou goest to possess it. The Lord shall smite thee with a consumption, and with a fever, and with an inflammation, and with an extreme burning, and with the sword, and with blasting, and with mildew; and they shall pursue thee until thou perish. And thy heaven that is over thy head shall be brass, and the earth that is under thee shall be iron. The Lord shall make the rain of thy land powder and dust: from heaven shall it come down upon thee, until thou be destroyed. The Lord shall cause thee to be smitten before thine enemies: thou shalt go out one way against them, and flee seven ways before them: and shalt be removed into all the kingdoms of the earth. And thy carcase shall be meat unto all fowls of the air, and unto the beasts of the earth, and no man shall fray them away. The Lord will smite thee with the botch of Egypt, and with the emerods, and with the scab, and with the itch, whereof thou canst not be healed. The Lord shall smite thee with madness, and blindness, and astonishment of heart: And thou shalt grope at noonday, as the blind gropeth in darkness, and thou shalt not

prosper in thy ways: and thou shalt be only oppressed and spoiled evermore, and no man shall save thee … Then the Lord will make thy plagues wonderful, and the plagues of thy seed, even great plagues, and of long continuance, and sore sicknesses, and of long continuance. Moreover he will bring upon thee all the diseases of Egypt, which thou wast afraid of; and they shall cleave unto thee. Also every sickness, and every plague, which is not written in the book of this law, them will the Lord bring upon thee, until thou be destroyed. (Deuteronomy 28:15–29, 59–61)

Reading these scriptures in light of what Jesus did on the cross was a sobering moment for me. Not just what Jesus had to go through on the cross but also the curse placed on Him. God saw Him as disgusting and detestable. When the sins of the world were placed on Jesus, they made God sick, so He cursed Jesus in that moment. That breaks my heart when I think about that. Then God totally turned His back on Him because Jesus was repulsive to look at. That's what it took for me to be blessed. For me to have everything He is, He had to take my place, my cursing, for me to have His blessing. That's the trade. This brought me to a place where I needed to appreciate what Christ had done for me. I should honor Him with my life. He deserves my obedience and all my worship. Forgive me, Lord, for my lack of humility and honor to You. I must value this. I must admire this. I must allow this reality of what took place to sink in.

…I am come that they might have life, and that they might have it more abundantly. (John 10:10)

Jesus saith unto him, I am the way, the truth, and the life: no man cometh unto the Father, but by me. (John 14:6)

He didn't come just so we would have *a* life or just to have life but to give us Life (Himself) and be our Bridegroom. All the scriptures in Jeremiah and Isaiah that talk about being decked with gold and precious stones and fine linens—everything that represents beauty and the beautifying of the house—come from our beloved Savior. Every bit of it comes from Him because He is giving us Himself. He is betrothing Himself to us. Everything He is, all of it, is ours! That's not what *I* am saying; that is what *He* is saying. The beauty you see and His kingdom are yours if you say yes to the proposal Jesus gives to be His bride. Jesus went to that well to break traditions and invite you in on everything He is and has for you.

How can you say no to the King of glory asking you to be His bride? It is like the most popular guy in school asking you to be his. The greatest man to have ever walked this earth, who created this earth, the most powerful, strongest One who ever was and ever will be just

asked you to be His. Why would you say no? How can we resist such an invitation? Oh, how I love Him!

> And there was delivered unto him the book of the prophet Esaias. And when he had opened the book, he found the place where it was written, The Spirit of the Lord is upon me, because he hath anointed me to preach the gospel to the poor; he hath sent me to heal the brokenhearted, to preach deliverance to the captives, and recovering of sight to the blind, to set at liberty them that are bruised, to preach the acceptable year of the Lord. And he closed the book, and he gave it again to the minister, and sat down. And the eyes of all them that were in the synagogue were fastened on him. And he began to say unto them, This day is this scripture fulfilled in your ears. (Luke 4:17–21)

> To appoint unto them that mourn in Zion, to give unto them beauty for ashes, the oil of joy for mourning, the garment of praise for the spirit of heaviness; that they might be called trees of righteousness, the planting of the Lord, that he might be glorified. (Isaiah 61:3)

Give Jesus your ashes, and He will give you His beauty. Give Jesus your mourning, tears, and hurt, and He will anoint you with the oil of joy. Give Jesus your spirit of heaviness, and He will give you the garment of praise. What a beautiful trade indeed!

> And he answered and spake unto those that stood before him, saying, Take away the filthy garments from him. And unto him he said, Behold, I have caused thine iniquity to pass from thee, and I will clothe thee with change of raiment. (Zechariah 3:4)

He wants to prove Himself as a sure reality in the details of our lives if we would only take the time and make the time to spend with Him and talk with Him every morning. Show me someone who is full of the joy of the Lord, and I will show you what the beautifying of the house of the Lord looks like. It is what He longs for—that you would put on that robe of righteousness that has joy and peace and love stitched all throughout it and walk in Him. And in keeping the Word, there isn't just a reward but a *great* reward.

> But without faith it is impossible to please him: for he that cometh to God must believe that he is, and that he is a rewarder of them that diligently seek him. (Hebrew 11:6)

God is a rewarder of those who diligently seek Him, who seek His face, His Word, daily. They earnestly pray and ask the Lord to use His Word to cut them open, to expose anything

that is in their house, His temple, that makes it ugly and repulsive to Him. It isn't the outer appearance of us that makes us beautiful; it is who is within us, Jesus, who makes us beautiful—something people will eventually see.

THE KING'S ROBE

There once was a king who lived long ago, whose kingdom prospered under his reign. Those within his kingdom lived a peaceful life. He wasn't a king who merely sat within his castle walls, but he was among his people.

One day, while riding his royal horse through one of the many towns of his land, he noticed a young boy sitting on the street. His clothes were torn, worn paper thin, and covered in dirt. He watched as the townspeople interacted with him. Some walked by, never paying attention to the child, while a few stopped and handed him a piece of bread or a cup of water before carrying on with what they were doing.

As he watched, he was moved with compassion for the boy. He dismounted his horse, walked over, and knelt before him. "Would you like to come with me?" the king asked as he reached out his hand. The boy looked at those standing around him as if seeking advice on what he was supposed to do. No one had ever invited him to go anywhere, and now here was the king extending the invitation. He looked into the face of the king. His eyes were gentle, and his smile was warm, comforting, and genuine. The boy managed to utter a trembling "Yes" as he reached out and took the king's hand.

The king helped the boy stand to his feet, placed him on his royal horse, and walked beside him all the way back to the castle. Before the sun set that evening, the king had a royal room prepared for the boy, and a seat was set for him at the king's table next to the king. A servant was assigned to the boy, who assisted in giving him new apparel fit for his new life of royalty.

That evening, there was a ceremony in which the king adopted the boy as His son, making him the prince of the kingdom. The king motioned to his servants, and they brought forth a robe and handed it to the king. "This is my robe, and today I have adopted you as my son; therefore, this is now your robe for you to wear so that all who see you will know that you are my son, the son of the king." And the king placed his robe on the boy.

Every morning, the servant of the new prince woke him and helped him get ready for the day. As the servant was laying out the prince's attire, he watched the prince reach under his bed and pull out the torn, filthy garments the king had found him wearing. The prince put them on and stood before the mirror. Then he removed the old garment, dressed in his royal attire, along with the king's robe, stood before the mirror, and wept.

Confused, the servant asked the prince, "My lord, please forgive me, but I must know. Are you not happy wearing the royal attire and the king's robe?"

The prince turned around with tears streaming down his face and said, "Yes, of course I am happy! How could I not be?"

The servant pressed, "Then why is it that you still have your old, filthy garments? And why is it you weep when you put on the king's robe?"

The prince smiled so big as more tears welled up in his eyes and spilled down his cheeks. "So that I remember who I was when the king came to me and offered me a new life, because I don't ever want to forget what the king has done for me."

I love weddings. I am a sucker for all things wedding, and I have been that way since I was a little girl. I also love the hype before that beautiful day leading up to that final moment we have all been waiting for when the bride walks down the aisle to marry her groom.

My son Justin was married this year to my sweet, new daughter-in-law Hannah. Absolutely everything was a dream to watch. But if someone were to ask me my favorite moment of the wedding day, I would have to be honest and say it was watching my son's reaction to his bride walking down the aisle.

The music started to play, cuing Hannah's entrance, and every eye shifted to the back of the room, but my eyes stayed on my son. The moment the song started her journey to Justin, he looked up, gasped with a deep breath, and began to cry with complete joy. This led him to clap his hands over and over. If anyone knows Justin, they know he isn't ashamed to express his emotion, whatever that emotion may be. The scene was so captivating that I couldn't take my eyes off the joy on his face. Hannah was finally about to be his bride!

One day soon there will be another bride ready to wed her groom. This bride is arrayed with fine, white linen dripping with righteousness and beauty placed on her from her heavenly Husband! We are that bride, the church. Can you imagine with me for one second what it will be like when we finally see our Jesus face-to-face? I try to imagine the moment our eyes will

meet, remembering all the times I spent with Him at His feet, reading His Word and praying. Now our faith will become sight. What a glorious day that will be when we see our Bridegroom, King Jesus! But all eyes will be on Him, for He is the One worthy of it all.

> Let us be glad and rejoice, and give honour to him: for the marriage of the Lamb is come, and his wife hath made herself ready. (Revelation 19:7)

May we never forget what the King did for us.

> For he hath made him to be sin for us, who knew no sin; that we might be made the righteousness of God in him. (2 Corinthians 5:21)

One day there will be a wedding.

> Blessed is he whose transgression is forgiven, whose sin is covered. (Psalm 32:1)

Jesus, I am overwhelmed in this moment as the truth of what You did for me washes over me. You became sin, You were made a curse, and You died so I may not only live but also be forgiven. I am now covered and clothed in Your righteousness. Wow! What a trade! I am so unworthy to be clothed in You. Let me never forget what You have done for me. From this day forward, help me to live a life worthy of the robe You have placed on me. Help me to cherish and value You, Jesus. Thank You for the blood that has redeemed my soul and given me this relationship with You. I love You, Lord. In Jesus's name.

Beloved, you are wanted.

You are adorned.

GROUP DISCUSSION QUESTIONS

A: Adorn

Blessed be the Lord God of our fathers, which hath put such a thing as this in the king's heart, to beautify the house of the Lord which is in Jerusalem: (Ezra 7:27)

What comes to mind when you know that Jesus not only desires a relationship with you but also wants to make you beautiful with His robe of righteousness?

_____
_____
_____
_____
_____
_____

`Righteousness: Blamelessness, innocence, justification.`

What scriptures come to mind after reading the definition of "righteousness"?

_____
_____
_____
_____
_____

What came to mind as you read Deuteronomy 28:2–14 about the blessings of God we now have because of Jesus?

_____
_____
_____
_____
_____

What came to mind as you read Deuteronomy 28:15–29, 59–61 about the cursing laid on Jesus for us to become His?

_____

_____

_____

_____

_____

_____

How do you feel about the truth that you are now beautiful in God's sight because of our Savior?

_____

_____

_____

_____

_____

_____

CHAPTER 7

WANTED

N: NURTURE

N: NURTURE

Jesus wants to *nurture* you.

He is your Bread of Life.

Nurture: That which promotes growth; education; instruction. To feed; to nourish. To educate; to bring or train up.[13]

God is our Father, and He is an expert at being a father. He is a hands-on God, and His priority is to grow us up in Jesus. He desires to strengthen us, comfort us, teach us, and nurture us. This is His character. It is who He is and all He does.

> The Lord is my strength and song, and he is become my salvation: he is my God, and I will prepare him an habitation; my father's God, and I will exalt him. (Exodus 15:2)

How does this work? How are we strengthened and nourished by God? The answer is by His Word, who Jesus is. It always goes back to the Word, to the beginning. It is always Jesus. We must take John 1:1 as sure reality. He has so much for us, and it is His nature to feed us, to give us nourishment not only spiritually but also physically. Don't take my word for it; take His.

> Behold, I will bring it health and cure, and I will cure them, and will reveal unto them the abundance of peace and truth. (Jeremiah 33:6)

> The thief cometh not, but for to steal, and to kill, and to destroy: but I am come that they might have life, and that they might have it more abundantly. (John 10:10)

When we align our thoughts to the Word of God and do what it says, the outcome will be health and healing. Whatever goes in is what comes out. Choose to do what the Word says, and it will produce the effect of health for all your flesh.

> Behold the fowls of the air: for they sow not, neither do they reap, nor gather into barns; yet your heavenly Father feedeth them. Are ye not much better than they? (Matthew 6:26)

As simple as this may sound, Jesus didn't die for the birds, yet He feeds them every single day. However, Jesus did die for *you*. His desire is toward *you*. He has given you more than a meal or two throughout the day, He has given you the Bread of Life. He has given you

Himself. Everything He is, everything He has, He has freely given to you. All you have to do it is accept it.

Have you ever noticed when the birds are most active in eating? It's in the morning. But not just in the morning; it's early in the morning. I believe this illustration is significant. The Lord could have used any other creature in this passage, but He chose birds. Why? God knows I am a visual learner, and He showed me His truth to help me understand the importance of receiving nourishment in the morning.

> And Moses said, Let no man leave of it till the morning. Notwithstanding they hearkened not unto Moses; but some of them left of it until the morning, and it bred worms, and stank: and Moses was wroth with them. And they gathered it every morning, every man according to his eating: and when the sun waxed hot, it melted. (Exodus 16:19–21)

First, we need to start with the manna. The Lord provided food for the Israelites by sending down manna from heaven every morning. They were to gather just enough for what was needed for that day, which, by the way, was always enough. If they were greedy and took too much for themselves, like the scripture says in Exodus, the extra became worm filled and stank.

God still provides manna from heaven today. That Manna is Jesus. He is the Bread of Life sent down from heaven for us. Again, the Word is Jesus Christ, and the way we are nourished with exactly what we need for each day is by being *in* the Word every morning. Our Father knows what is needed, and He wants to nurture us with the exact thing we will need for today. We can be strengthened and encouraged; know the peace of God in every situation and finish the day in Him with joy because God nourished us with His strength, encouragement, and peace—which is who He is.

Get your Bible out, and let's look at more scripture about the significance of meeting with our Father in the morning.

- Exodus 34:1–2
- Psalm 5:3
- Psalm 90:6
- Proverbs 8:17
- Lamentations 3:22–24

New mercies are given in the morning because our minds are fresh and ready to receive the nourishment for that day. God knows what we need before we ask, and when we seek Him early, we receive what we need. That's a promise from Him.

Is this house, which is called by my name, become a den of robbers in your eyes? Behold, even I have seen it, saith the Lord … And now, because ye have done all these works, saith the Lord, and I spake unto you, rising up early and speaking, but ye heard not; and I called you, but ye answered not. (Jeremiah 7:11, 13)

Precious one, it is time we stop ignoring the voice of our Father when He calls us to meet with Him early. I know it upsets me when I call for my children and they ignore me, knowing that they heard me. Why do we think it would be any different with the Lord? When the Creator, almighty God, speaks to us, especially during the first parts of our day, it is for our good, and what He wants to tell us is vital and important for what lies ahead of us that we cannot see. And I promise He will give you the strength and endurance to make it through the day, no matter how much sleep you lack from the night before, because His Word is nourishment. It is the energy our literal bodies need.

Then Jesus said unto them, Verily, verily, I say unto you, Moses gave you not that bread from heaven; but my Father giveth you the true bread from heaven. For the bread of God is he which cometh down from heaven, and giveth life unto the world. Then said they unto him, Lord, evermore give us this bread. And Jesus said unto them, I am the bread of life: he that cometh to me shall never hunger; and he that believeth on me shall never thirst. (John 6:32–35)

Jesus is the Bread of Life. He is not only our drink but also our food. We will never hunger or thirst again. This is how we live the abundant life. Jesus supplies everything we will ever need or be in want of. Daily bread is the representation of our daily relationship with Him, and He is enough.

According as his divine power hath given unto us all things that pertain unto life and godliness, through the knowledge of him that hath called us to glory and virtue. (2 Peter 1:3)

What happens to the child of God who isn't being fed and nourished by the Word of God? They will be in a spiritual drought and become hardened and calloused by anything that is of God. They will hear the Word of God and be numb to it.

Harden not your heart, as in the provocation, and as in the day of temptation in the wilderness. (Psalm 95:8)

Sow to yourselves in righteousness, reap in mercy; break up your fallow ground:
for it is time to seek the Lord, till he come and rain righteousness upon you.
(Hosea 10:12)

Many of us return to God, and if there is no *feeling* of change, we stop and wind up in the same boat where we started; cold, hardened, and calloused. We must get desperate with Him and for Him, shutting ourselves in with Him until He does affect us.

Sometimes I get weary from life. Weary from pain. Weary from simply doing the right thing. I get weary of going to church each Sunday, making sure the kids are up ready for school each morning during the week and making sure they are fed and lunches are made, all the while trying to hold it together emotionally. I get weary of praying, doing devotionals with them each morning, and making sure everyone and everything is taken care of. Is it just me, or is it getting harder to stay focused on *why* we do what we do? Can I ring a bell and say, "I am done! Mom needs a break"? But I know all life and its chaos will still be waiting for me when I get done with being done. If that isn't enough, it takes only a second of watching the news or scrolling through social media to realize how much of a mess our country and the world are in. It just seems like it's getting harder to stay focused on Jesus, His Word, and why we are created.

When I am distracted, I no longer rely on the Word, which gives me strength and endurance to face life; and I get weary, just like we do when we skip a meal. Our bodies need food to produce the energy needed throughout the day. I get so frustrated with myself because I can be so easily distracted from the One I need to get through each day. I just want to encourage you to keep going. Keep seeking the One who is all you will ever need and want in this life. Keep your eyes on Jesus. This is when it counts the most, when it's hard, when you want to give up. When it hurts more than anything. When no one else is standing, keep standing. When it seems like everything and everyone is coming at you, don't look away from Him. Rely on Jesus. Depend on His Word. Seek it as you would if your literal body was desperate for energy, strength, and nourishment. God is for you, not against you. His Word is enough to keep you steady until He calls you home. Nothing else can promise that, and even if it did, it would fail and leave you lacking because it is a counterfeit. No one can satisfy and fulfill us like Jesus, the Word of God.

What are the things you indulge in that are gradually taking the place of the Bread of Heaven? Don't rush through this question. Stop for a moment and seriously ask the Holy Spirit to reveal what the thing is that is blocking and robbing you of the needed nourishment of the Word.

SO WHAT CAN GOD'S WORD, THE BREAD OF LIFE (JESUS), DO FOR ME?

1. His Word is like a fire and hammer, which will break the hardness of my heart and burn away what isn't of Him, not to punish me. But like a refiner's fire, it will refine me so I will look more and more like Jesus.

> Is not my word like as a fire? saith the Lord; and like a hammer that breaketh the rock in pieces? (Jeremiah 23:29)

2. His Word feeds me and keeps me alive.

> And Jesus answered him, saying, It is written, That man shall not live by bread alone, but by every word of God. (Luke 4:4)

3. His Word gives me joy.

> Thy words were found, and I did eat them; and thy word was unto me the joy and rejoicing of mine heart: for I am called by thy name, O Lord God of hosts. (Jeremiah 15:16)

4. His Word is powerful and sharp, able to cut away the things stunting my growth in Him.

> For the word of God is quick, and powerful, and sharper than any twoedged sword, piercing even to the dividing asunder of soul and spirit, and of the joints and marrow, and is a discerner of the thoughts and intents of the heart. (Hebrews 4:12)

5. His Word comforts me. (Have you ever heard of "comfort food?" Ha! He is your spiritual comfort food.)

> Neither have I gone back from the commandment of his lips; I have esteemed the words of his mouth more than my necessary food. (Job 23:12)

6. His Word is sweeter than the honeycomb.

> The law of the Lord is perfect, converting the soul: the testimony of the Lord is sure, making wise the simple. The statutes of the Lord are right, rejoicing the heart: the commandment of the Lord is pure, enlightening the eyes. The fear of the Lord is clean, enduring for ever: the judgments of the Lord are true

and righteous altogether. More to be desired are they than gold, yea, than much fine gold: sweeter also than honey and the honeycomb. Moreover by them is thy servant warned: and in keeping of them there is great reward. (Psalm 19:7–11)

7. His Word heals me and delivers me from destruction.

He sent his word, and healed them, and delivered them from their destructions. (Psalm 107:20)

8. His Word gives me wisdom and understanding.

Open thou mine eyes, that I may behold wondrous things out of thy law. (Psalm 119:18)

Give me understanding, and I shall keep thy law; yea, I shall observe it with my whole heart. (Psalm 119:34)

9. His Word sustains and protects me from affliction and from becoming apathetic.

Apathetic: Void of feeling; free from passion; insensible.[14]

Unless thy law had been my delights, I should then have perished in my affliction. I will never forget thy precepts: for with them thou hast quickened me. (Psalm 119:92–93)

Numb. Life gets busy. And it doesn't stop when pain and circumstances happen. I personally believe that when life gets this way, emotional pain and physical hurt intensifies. So, we detach—and then we become numb.

And isn't it safe to say that we buy the lie, that it's just easier this way? Because, if I am around people then I have to "pretend" and "lie" that everything is okay—when it's not. I also think we fuel this emotional callous by indulging our flesh. Letting ourselves be daily overstimulated by the things of this world. Our senses are in overdrive. And then we crash emotionally and physically.

We are not made to handle this much, and the enemy loves it. We know and have read that he wants to kill, steal, and destroy us. This isn't a new teaching. (John 10:10) But we still embrace this emotional solitary confinement. And if that pain isn't enough, the physical pain we experience also feeds the plague of spiritual paralysis. It hurts to move. Again, because when we move we are reminded of what brought us here. We've bought the lie, and now, we are addicted to the numb.

But then, something just tells you to grab His Word, and not the remote.

> He sent his word, and healed them… (Psalm 107:20)

> For they are life unto those that find them, and health to all their flesh. (Proverbs 4:22)

> Is not my word like as a fire? saith the Lord; and like a hammer that breaketh the rock in pieces? (Jeremiah 23:29)

His Word that is life and truth begins to crush and break through the thick wall you spent years to build. Hammering and chiseling the calloused barrier to the heart He longs to heal and change. It hurts, but you begin to embrace His healing. He cuts out the lies that are mortared around the one thing He bought, melting the ice that has made you numb. Knowing that the moment He speaks His Words it will bring health and healing to all your flesh! It will produce life into all your body! Your mind! Before you know it, Jesus, the Word of God has awakened, restored, renewed, and brought healing and life back into your bones again!

And you will say trembling…

> …Lord, to whom shall we go? thou hast the words of eternal life. (John 6:68)

Where else can I go? Just give me Jesus. His Word amazes me.

10. His Word gives me a love for Him and less love for the things of the world.

> It is time for thee, Lord, to work: for they have made void thy law. Therefore I love thy commandments above gold; yea, above fine gold. Therefore I esteem all thy precepts concerning all things to be right; and I hate every false way. (Psalm 119:126–128)

11. His Word helps me understand His Word.

> The entrance of thy words giveth light; it giveth understanding unto the simple. (Psalm 119:130)

12. His Word gives me a burden for the ungodly.

> Rivers of waters run down mine eyes, because they keep not thy law. (Psalm 119:136)

13. His Word gives me peace, and I won't be offended by what others think or say about me. Many of us get our feelings hurt because truthfully we care more about what people think than

about what God thinks. Someone who loves God's Word, studies it, and lives it will reflect a life of peace. Those who live in this peace, that only God can provide, won't be offended by what others say or how they are treated because they know *whose* they are. This is a good way to gauge our growth *in* Him.

> Great peace have they which love thy law: and nothing shall offend them. (Psalm 119:165)

14. His Word gives me faith.

> So then faith cometh by hearing, and hearing by the word of God. (Romans 10:17)

At a young age, I was taught to memorize the Word of God, but it was never that important to me until August 16, 2003. In addition to the stories I was taught in Sunday school, I had also read stories of Christians giving their lives to be tortured for Jesus, and they filled me with questions. *What makes people live and die like this? Let alone not care about what people think about them? Why don't I have that kind of walk? Why don't I have that kind of love for Jesus?* The answer the Lord spoke to my heart was simple yet powerfully life changing. The answer was an invitation to get to know Him intimately.

The Bible contains the mind of God. It contains the nourishment we need.

> And Jesus answered him, saying, It is written, That man shall not live by bread alone, but by every word of God. (Luke 4:4)

Dear Father, I know I cannot live on bread alone but by every Word out of Your mouth. I know that the bread from heaven in the Word of God You have preserved for me to know Your mind. To know You. Help me to hunger and thirst for You and You alone. Help me to lay down the things in my life that have taken the place of Your nourishment that I need and desire. Lord, I desire to know You, to come closer. Increase the desire even more. Thank You for providing for my needs, for being a good Father to me and never letting me go. I love you, Lord. In Jesus's name.

Beloved, you are wanted.

You are nurtured.

GROUP DISCUSSION QUESTIONS

N: Nurture

Behold the fowls of the air: for they sow not, neither do they reap, nor gather into barns; yet your heavenly Father feedeth them. Are ye not much better than they? (Matthew 6:26)

What are some scriptures that tell us God the Father wants to nurture us?

_____

_____

_____

_____

_____

_____

_____

Do you believe the Lord _wants_ to take care of you? Why or why not?

_____

_____

_____

_____

_____

_____

_____

Of the list of fourteen things the Word can do for us, which ones have you experienced the most? Which ones do you struggle with?

_____

_____

_____

_____

_____

_____

_____

Do you think it's important for you to spend time with God in the morning? Why or why not?

_____

_____

_____

_____

_____

_____

Read 2 Peter 1:3. What are some other scriptures that prove a relationship with Jesus, the Bread of Life, is enough?

_____

_____

_____

_____

_____

_____

CHAPTER 8

WANTED

T: TEACH

T: TEACH

Jesus wants to *teach* you.

He is your Teacher.

`Teach: To educate, instruct, coach, train, enlighten, guide, show, instruct, edify, indoctrinate,` *`discipline`*`.`[15]

In my mind, I have always pictured a teacher as someone who stands in the front of a classroom lecturing from a book and occasionally writing something on a chalkboard. I wasn't expecting a teacher to be one who also disciplines.

> That the trial of your faith, being much more precious than of gold that perisheth, though it be tried with fire, might be found unto praise and honor and glory at the appearing of Jesus Christ. (1 Peter 1:7)

Teachers are also known to give tests and the dreaded pop quizzes when we aren't expecting them. The purpose of God testing and *trying* our faith is to make us look more like Jesus. These trials aren't easy, but there is always a reason for them. That reason is to glorify His name in and through us and for our good, to strengthen our faith *in* Him and Him alone. There is a purpose for the pain.

One example of a *pop quiz* in my life was in 2000. Micheal and I were expecting another child. We were so excited and were hoping for a baby brother for Brianne and Justin. If it was a girl, that would be okay too. Late one night I experienced intense pain and began to go into labor. At twenty-one weeks, we lost our baby. I chose not to know whether it was a boy or girl because it was too hard to bear. My doctor performed the D&C, and shortly after my recovery, we moved. For the next seven years, we tried to get pregnant again, but each year went by, and my issue became only worse.

In 2007 we moved because my husband was given a job promotion that offered amazing benefits and insurance for the whole family. At the time I was dealing with some intense physical issues that landed me to see three different doctors. All of them eventually told me I could never have any more children and would need surgery to stop the pain. Devastated by this news, we scheduled the surgery. After three months in a new town with a new job, a new house, a new doctor, and a new church, my husband got fired. What in the world were we going to do? I was still in excruciating pain, but now no insurance meant no surgery. We had two kids to feed but no income. How would we survive? No one knew us here because we had just

moved. I knew the Lord had brought us here, but the questions and doubts began to surface nonetheless. Did we misunderstand His leading to move here? If not, why would He bring us to a new place and just take it all away?

I knew God had healed and provided for people in the Bible stories I had read as a child. I had seen this happen for friends and family members, so I grabbed His Word for answers. These were the scriptures that gave me the faith I needed in Him. This was clearly my opportunity to trust God.

> Thou wilt keep him in perfect peace, whose mind is stayed on thee: because he trusteth in thee. Trust ye in the Lord for ever: for in the Lord Jehovah is everlasting strength: (Isaiah 26:3–4)

> Remember ye not the former things, neither consider the things of old. Behold, I will do a new thing; now it shall spring forth; shall ye not know it? I will even make a way in the wilderness, and rivers in the desert. (Isaiah 43:18–19)

> Let your conversation be without covetousness; and be content with such things as ye have: for he hath said, I will never leave thee, nor forsake thee. So that we may boldly say, The Lord is my helper, and I will not fear what man shall do unto me. (Hebrews 13:5–6)

It was time we fully trusted that God would do what He had promised. Micheal quickly found work, and we found a good church to go to where we began to meet new friends, but the pain was still intense and unbearable at times.

One morning I was reading my daily devotional. The scripture reference was in Mark 5.

> And a certain woman, which had an issue of blood twelve years, and had suffered many things of many physicians, and had spent all that she had, and was nothing bettered, but rather grew worse, when she had heard of Jesus, came in the press behind, and touched his garment. For she said, If I may touch but his clothes, I shall be whole. And straightway the fountain of her blood was dried up; and she felt in her body that she was healed of that plague. And Jesus, immediately knowing in himself that virtue had gone out of him, turned him about in the press, and said, Who touched my clothes? And he looked round about to see her that had done this thing. But the woman fearing and trembling, knowing what was done in her, came and fell down before him, and told him all the truth. And he said unto her, Daughter, thy faith hath made thee whole; go in peace, and be whole of thy plague. (Mark 5:25–30, 32–34)

After I finished reading this story, I asked the Lord, *Would You do that for me? Would You stop the bleeding and the pain? I know You can, but would You?*

I started getting ready for church, and on the way there, I heard a new song on the radio, "One Touch" by Nicole C. Mullen. If you don't already know it, it's about the woman with the issue of blood. The same story I had just read about that morning was now being told on the radio by a song! Later on the same day, I went to help our church feed the homeless at a window repair car shop. There were about thirty people there. After the music, the missions pastor started reading out of Luke 8:43–48.

As I listened, I realized it was the same story I had read that morning and heard sung on the radio. Now the missions pastor was preaching it. My heart was full of emotion and anticipation. I knew God was answering the question I had asked Him earlier that morning. The pastor stopped midsentence and said, "Someone is in here right now who wants to be healed. Press through the crowd and let us pray with you." I knew it was me. Uncontrollably weeping, embarrassed, and trembling, I walked up and asked for prayer. The missions pastor, a deacon, and a sister saint anointed me with oil and prayed for me.

The pain immediately left me. I couldn't wait to get home and tell Micheal. We saw God move and provide countless times in the season of job loss and disease. God was faithful. Three months after being healed, I was pregnant with our youngest son, Levi. We made forever and lasting friendships with the members of Harmony Hill Baptist Church. God used many of them to teach me how to pray and to take God at His Word. Lufkin, Texas, will always hold such a special place in my heart.

A job loss doesn't change who God is. Circumstances and tribulations don't change the promises He has given. A worldwide pandemic doesn't change the purpose of His plans for you and your life. There's nothing that could ever happen that changes His Word.

For ever, O Lord, thy word is settled in heaven. (Psalm 119:89)

So then faith cometh by hearing, and hearing by the word of God. (Romans 10:17)

Consistency in the Word fuels faith. Consistency in the world and its views fuels fear. What is fueling you? What if the trial and pain are there for God to show up and perform a miracle in your life? Trust Him.

For the Lord will not cast off for ever: but though he cause grief, yet will he have compassion according to the multitude of his mercies. (Lamentations 3:31–32)

1. Testing is for our good.

> My brethren, count it all joy when ye fall into divers temptations; knowing this, that the trying of your faith worketh patience. (James 1:2–3)

> And not only so, but we glory in tribulations also: knowing that tribulation worketh patience; and patience, experience; and experience, hope: and hope maketh not ashamed; because the love of God is shed abroad in our hearts by the Holy Ghost which is given unto us. (Romans 5:3-5)

2. Testing is our chance to be obedient to God and allow His character to be built in us.

> He must increase, but I must decrease. (John 3:30)

3. Testing is designed to strengthen our commitment to obey no matter what.

> There hath no temptation taken you but such as is common to man: but God is faithful, who will not suffer you to be tempted above that ye are able; but will with the temptation also make a way to escape, that ye may be able to bear it. (1 Corinthians 10:13)

4. Testing also comes to prove our walk and love for our God.

> Thou shalt not hearken unto the words of that prophet, or that dreamer of dreams: for the Lord your God proveth you, to know whether ye love the Lord your God with all your heart and with all your soul. (Deuteronomy 13:3)

I love the Greek definition for the word *prove*.

Dokimazo (dok-im-ad'-zo); I put to the test, I prove, I examine, I distinguish by testing, approve that I am fit.[16]

> Examine me, O Lord, and prove me; try my reins and my heart. For thy lovingkindness is before mine eyes: and I have walked in thy truth. (Psalm 26:2–3)

Take a moment, put pen to paper, and write out a time in your life you know God designed to prove your love for Him.

_____

_____

_____

_____

_____

_____

_____

Our God is a hands-on God. He desires to make you more like Jesus. You can either embrace this plan or go to the woodshed until you do. I promise that every trial, pain, betrayal, struggle, and hurt is intended for a purpose or plan that has been intricately woven together to fit your life for His glory. The God of the Old Testament temple, with all its details, is the God of this temple right here and now. You, the one He bought with the precious blood of Jesus Christ, are being perfected and refined for His glory.

Sometimes we put a negative spin on trials, blaming them all on the devil, when it's the Lord who is allowing the testing. Don't get me wrong; the enemy does attack us, but nothing leaves the desk of God without His stamp of approval. *We are His!*

"Singing is my passion!" "Teaching is my passion" "Preaching is my passion!" I have heard or even said these things one or more times over the years, but what I have come to learn is that when we grab hold of a real, intimate relationship with Jesus Christ, when we know Him for Him, not what He does, everything changes, including our passions. When we seek His face, His presence, we find that nothing else can come close to comparison. Jesus becomes that fiery passion we crave, and He is what fuels everything we do. Then our statement changes from a *thing* being our passion to Jesus, who is our passion. It won't matter what we do. If our passion is Christ, there will be a joy unspeakable, a radiance and shine about us, and all we do and say will glorify our Savior, even if it is cleaning toilets and folding laundry. It isn't the thing that now drives us. It is the King of glory!

The first half of 2022 has had trials that have tested my faith. During my whole life, I have always loved to sing. In fact, my mom says I came out of the womb singing and haven't stopped since. So, when I was born again on August 16, 2003, it was easy for me to serve Jesus this way. It was natural for me to pour out my love, passion, devotion, and praise to Him with song. I served in different music ministries at my church—in the choir, praise team, ensembles, and presentational songs. I served wherever the Lord allowed me the opportunity to do so.

In 2020 I began to experience a deterioration in my vocal cords. I was the only one who seemed to notice the change in my sound and pitch at the time. It wasn't until 2022 that it really became apparent to others. This caused concern that there was possibly something going on with my voice. It would be heartbreaking to me, when I sang a song to Jesus, and only air came out instead of a sound. Fearful of what I was about to hear, I finally decided to go to the

doctor and see what was going on. Sure enough, the scope revealed nodules, and damage to my vocal cords. I needed to be placed on vocal-singing rest.

I'm not going to lie; this season has been trying for me, and I'm not sure how long it will last. But two things have come from this trial. First, no one can ever take my song because Jesus is my Song (Isaiah 12:2). He is enough for me. Second, He is using this trial to show me that He doesn't want to just *sing* His Word; he wants to *speak* His Word. A few years ago, I saw a cartoon drawing of a little girl that spoke volumes to me. She is maybe five years old, has brown hair, and is standing before Jesus. She is looking down and tightly grasping a small, worn, torn teddy bear. The caption above her says, "But I love it so much." Jesus is smiling, lovingly holding out one hand to her while asking her to give the bear to Him. What the little girl can't see is that behind His back, Jesus is holding onto a new, life-size teddy bear He is ready and willing to give to her, but before He will, she has to give Him what is precious to her, the small, old, worn, and very torn teddy bear.

I gave Jesus my voice a long time ago, but it wasn't until it actually left me that I truly realized He had new and bigger plans for me beyond what I could possibly imagine. I fully believe the Lord can restore my vocal cords, but if He chooses not to, I am satisfied in knowing that I'm not my own, that my life is His life. I'm content with Him and whatever He chooses to do.

> I will go and return to my place, till they acknowledge their offence, and seek my face: in their affliction they will seek me early. (Hosea 5:15)

> Come, and let us return unto the Lord: for he hath torn, and he will heal us; he hath smitten, and he will bind us up. (Hosea 6:1)

> When thou sadist, Seek my face; my heart said unto thee, Thy face, Lord, will I seek. (Psalm 27:8)

5. Testing comes to keep us from going astray.

> Before I was afflicted I went astray: but now have I kept thy word. (Psalm 119:67)

> It is good for me that I have been afflicted; that I might learn thy statutes. (Psalm 119:71)

God sent the Holy Spirit to teach, guide, and comfort us in, by, and through the Word.

> Howbeit when he, the Spirit of truth, is come, he will guide you into all truth: for he shall not speak of himself; but whatsoever he shall hear, that shall he speak: and he will shew you things to come. (John 16:13)

6. Testing comes so we may *know* Him more.

> Yea doubtless, and I count all thing but loss for the excellency of the knowledge of Christ Jesus my Lord: for whom I have suffered the loss of all things, and do count them but dung, that I may win Christ. (Philippians 3:8)

Do these scriptures stir your heart? To *know* Him is more precious than anything. If trials and testing come so I may know Him more, then friend, they are worth it. That is what Paul is saying here in Philippians 3. Oh, to *know* Him and to be *known* by Him!

For two weeks during my time with the Lord in the mornings, Psalm 27:8, Psalm 108:1, and Hebrews 12:1 repeatedly came up. Some stresses and lies from my past were taking place that the enemy still uses to cause me to doubt and shift my focus. It wasn't only in the moments in my prayer closet but throughout the days too. I was reminded of a song, or someone said something that caused me to recall these scriptures, or the scriptures themselves came to my mind and heart. Each time was a reminder to keep my eyes on Jesus despite all the distractions surrounding me.

One Sunday morning I was singing a duet with a friend of mine at church, and I will confess that I was consumed with the lies of the enemy. I was looking at those things, and my gaze was not on Jesus, where it needed to be. What I'm about to tell you may seem silly to some, but I want to share with you what the Lord did for me that morning. The moment I got on stage to practice the song, there were sudden changes in my eyesight. Everything was blurry, and I couldn't read the words on the large screen on the back wall. I will admit that I began to panic a little. I said something to a close friend of mine after practice, and she prayed for me. I continued to blink repeatedly, hoping that my vision would suddenly reappear or make itself right, but it was to no avail, and my vision remained hazy and blurry as the service began.

Since I couldn't see the words, I tried to simply think about the lyrics to the presentation song we would soon sing. That was a battle in and of itself. The lyrics caused my focus to shift to Jesus, but then I realized I still couldn't read the words, and my prayers turned to a desperate plea for help. The service started and the congregation began to sing praises to the King and my desperate prayers began to cease. My focus began to settle on Jesus alone. I may have lost the physical capability to focus on anything, but because of it, my spiritual focus became crystal clear. It is always about Him and will be forever about Him. His glory. His name. That morning, Jesus was the only One in that audience during the duet. He is all I saw, and He was all who mattered. The moment I sat down from singing, my vision returned to normal as if nothing had happened. The blurriness was gone!

He definitely taught me a lesson that Sunday morning that I won't soon forget, and I want to give Him glory and praise for what He did and maybe encourage others to turn their eyes upon Jesus. You know the hymn; it is playing in your mind right now. Look at Him! Let His face cause everything else around you to fade into the background.

7. Testing is my opportunity to rejoice. What do I do when it's just too hard or hurts too much? Rejoice!

> Beloved, think it not strange concerning the fiery trial which is to try you, as though some strange thing happened unto you: but rejoice, inasmuch as ye are partakers of Christ's suffering; that, when his glory shall be revealed, ye may be glad also with exceeding joy. (1 Peter 4:12–13)

Turn in your Bible to Psalm 107. As you read it, pay attention to how God created the trials and how He came through for them in each one.

When my youngest son was five years old, he asked me whether he could give the devil the "bad finger." I did my best not to burst into laughter and join him in the effort, but I knew this was a teachable moment, so I seized it. First, I needed to ask him how he knew about the "bad finger" and why he wanted to give it to the devil. Once those questions were answered, God spoke to my heart, and this is what came out.

"Levi, God didn't create a bad finger. He created you from head to toe and called it good. The devil wants you to lash out, scream, and complain about how he made you feel in this situation. Do you want the devil to leave you alone? Then take every one of those fingers God gave you, raise them toward heaven, and praise the Lord with your whole heart until you feel it in your bones. The devil hates that!"

So, with his sweet little voice, he started singing his favorite song, "Forever Reign," by Hillsong.

Dear one, it is freeing when we praise the Lord. If God inhabits the praises of His people and in His presence I will experience the fullness of joy, then why don't we praise Him in the storm? Why don't we call on the name of the Lord?

> Oh that men would praise the Lord for his goodness, and for his wonderful works to the children of men! (Psalm 107:8, 15, 21, 31)

> Thou wilt shew me the path of life: in thy presence is fullness of joy; at thy right hand there are pleasures for evermore. (Psalm 16:11)

When God is praised, the enemy scatters. The enemy wants to stick around because he wants to occupy your mind and take over God's rightful place in your life. He wants you to focus on his workings and the stress, sickness, doubts, sadness, loneliness, hurts, disappointments, anxieties, addictions, dysfunctions, shame, guilt, and so forth. If he can get you to focus on the situation and circumstance of the storms and trials, then you won't have time to focus on the Word. You won't have the energy to praise the Lord in the trial and through the storm. You won't be able to remember whose you are in that moment because you are tied up in what you are feeling. So, if he can shift your gaze and take your eyes off Jesus, you won't have the opportunity to praise the Lord and watch the enemy flee.

Let's be honest for a second. When I'm in the heat of the trial, the flesh doesn't have any desire to praise the Lord. It wants to gripe, complain, be angry, be sad, isolate, gossip, and so forth. I don't *feel* like praising the Lord because the trial hurts. It's uncomfortable. It can seem heavy or scary. But we know, because God's Word says it and God cannot lie, that if we praise the Lord for who He is, He will inhabit that praise, and His character is joy, peace, love, goodness, and freedom. The very essence of Him walks into the trial, sits down, and begins to infect the situation; and suddenly, I begin to feel and experience the God who created me to worship and praise Him.

If you don't feel God, shut yourself up in the secret place with Him and stay there until you do. And when you go into your quiet place, don't just sit there. Praise His name! Praise Him for who He is. Put all your pain, hurt, disappointments, stresses, worries, and so forth in your left hand and close it. Take all your goals, dreams, desires, and visions God has given you; place them in your right hand and close it. Then raise both fists to the sky toward heaven, to your Father; now open them. What position are you in? It is the position of surrender, which is the position of praise and worship. That is the position we need to stay in to continuously praise Him. And the enemy hates that.

When we rejoice in the Lord, the enemy runs. He literally flees in terror.

> Let God arise, let his enemies be scattered: let them also that hate him flee before him. (Psalm 68:1)

When God is praised, walls are demolished, and enemy strongholds are taken over. Remember the story of Jericho?

> So the people shouted when the priests blew with the trumpets: and it came to pass, when the people heard the sound of the trumpet, and the people shouted with a great shout, that the wall fell down flat, so that the people went up into the city, every man straight before him, and they took the city. (Joshua 6:20)

When God is praised, chains are broken, and prisoners are set free.

> And at midnight Paul and Silas prayed, and sang praises unto God: and the prisoners heard them. And suddenly there was a great earthquake, so that the foundations of the prison were shaken: and immediately all the doors were opened, and every one's bands were loosed. (Acts 16:25–26)

> Let every thing that hath breath praise the Lord. Praise ye the Lord. (Psalm 150:6)

The Lord stands by you and strengthens you. Praise Him! He works in you to proclaim the Gospel. Praise Him! He works in you to use you to reach those who don't know Christ. Praise Him! He has faithfully delivered you and will deliver you again. Praise Him! He fights your battles for you. Praise Him! He restores what the enemy has taken away. Praise Him! He gives beauty for ashes. Praise Him! He gives life abundantly. Praise Him! He never leaves you or forsakes you. Praise Him! In whatever storm you are in, He is using it for your good. Praise Him! He will bring you safely into His presence in heaven. Praise Him! Everything is ultimately for His glory, both now and forever. Praise Him!

If you want the enemy out of your life, praise Him. Praise Him. Praise Him!

IF IT HAD NOT BEEN

BY ANGELA MORGAN

If it had not been for affliction,

I wouldn't know Him deeper.

If it had not been for adversity,

I wouldn't know His faithfulness.

If it had not been for the pain,

I wouldn't know Him as my Healer.

If it had not been for the famine,

I wouldn't know Him as the Bread of Life.

If it had not been for the desert,

I wouldn't know Him as the Living Water.

If it had not been for the loneliness,

I wouldn't know that He never leaves me or forsakes me.

If it had not been for the rejection,

I wouldn't know Him as my Comforter.

And if it had not been for the losses in my life,

I wouldn't know that *Jesus is enough* for me.

There are two times to praise Him: when you feel like it and when you don't. You don't want to miss the moment of teaching that comes in the trials, the testing, and the discipline. Embrace it.

> For thou are great, and doest wonderous things: thou art God alone. Teach me thy way, O Lord; I will walk in thy truth: unite my heart to fear thy name. (Psalm 86:10-11)

Lord, You are more than my words can say. Your greatness and faithfulness towards me are more than I can comprehend. You leave me in awe of You. Continue to teach me in Your Word by Your Holy Spirit. Help me to embrace the testing and trying of my faith and to seize the opportunity to praise You louder during those times. You are worthy of it all and worth my all. Help me to keep my eyes fixed on You and to trust Your leading as You guide me through each day. In Jesus's name.

Beloved, You are wanted.

You are taught.

GROUP DISCUSSION QUESTIONS

T: Teach

That the trial of your faith, being much more precious than of gold that perisheth, though it be tried with fire, might be found unto praise and honour and glory at the appearing of Jesus Christ:

(1 Peter 1:7)

What is your first (honest) reaction when trials come into your life?

_____

_____

_____

_____

_____

_____

When was the last trial of your faith? What was the outcome of it?

_____

_____

_____

_____

_____

_____

Do you believe that every hurt, tear, struggle, and betrayal is for your good and serves to give Him glory? Why or why not?

_____

_____

_____

_____

_____

What are some scriptures you can grab hold of now so when (not if) the trials come, you will be able to stand?

_____

_____

_____

_____

_____

_____

List some of the ways you can shift your focus from the trials or temptations and fix your eyes on Jesus.

_____

_____

_____

_____

_____

_____

CHAPTER 9

WANTED
E: EMPOWER

E: EMPOWER

Jesus wants to *empower* you.

He is all-powerful.

Empower: To give power to, to give power to *do* something, to make stronger, to equip.

The Greek word for "power" is *dunamis*.

Dunamis: force (literally or figuratively); specially, miraculous power.[17]

Dunamis is where we get the English word *dynamite*.

Every part of this study is about God's character, and He is power. It isn't something He just gives us from His hand, but it's who He is. Which is why we need to seek His face. It's all about seeking Him to *know* Him, not just to receive things from Him. In His presence I receive everything He gives me because He gives me Himself.

> This know also, that in the last days perilous times shall come. For men shall be lovers of their own selves, covetous, boasters, proud, blasphemers, disobedient to parents, unthankful, unholy, without natural affection, trucebreakers, false accusers, incontinent, fierce, despisers of those that are good, traitors, heady, highminded, lovers of pleasures more than lovers of God; having a form of godliness, but denying the power thereof: from such turn away. For of this sort are they which creep into houses, and lead captive silly women laden with sins, led away with divers lusts, ever learning, and never able to come to the knowledge of the truth. (2 Timothy 3:1–7)

Covetous: Excessively eager to obtain and possess; directed to money or goods.[18]

Boasters: One who boasts, glories, or vaunts ostentatiously.[19]

Blasphemer: One who speaks of God in impious and irreverent terms.[20]

Trucebreaker: One who violates a truce, covenant, or engagement.[21]

Incontinent: Not restraining in passions or appetites, particularly the sexual appetite; indulging lust without restraint or in violation of law; unchaste; lewd.[22]

Fierce: Vehement, violent, furious, savage, ravenous, easily enraged, eager to mischief as a fierce tyrant.[23]

Traitor: One who violates his or her allegiance and betrays his or her country; one who is guilty of treason; one who takes arms and levies war against his or her country; or one who aids an enemy in conquering his or her country. One who betrays trust.[24]

Heady: Rash, hasty, violent, disposed to rush forward in an enterprise without thought or deliberation, ungovernable.[25]

High minded: Proud, arrogant.[26]

This also goes back to the temple, realizing whose temple we are and acknowledging the truth that we have been bought with a price. By allowing all these things to creep into our houses, we become thieves, a fact that made Jesus angry back in Mark 11. When we don't cast them out of our lives, we aren't watered; we are treating the robe of righteousness carelessly and dragging it through the mud, and we aren't nurtured or taught. We aren't valuing the relationship with Jesus because we aren't seeking Him.

Many of us have denied the power of the Holy Spirit and allowed different lusts to creep in and take over. And they aren't always the *bad* things we tend to think of. They could be busyness, family, and friends. They could be ministry and the work we do for the Lord that have crept in and taken priority in our lives instead of Jesus alone. We cannot be strong Christians if we aren't spending time in the Word, which is our power source.

The child of God who doesn't spend time in the Word and prayer will be a powerless and weak Christian, one easily swayed when tempted by ungodly things. Spending time with Him will empower you to fight your flesh and live a holy and upright life.

I can do all things through Christ which strengtheneth me. (Philippians 4:13)

That he would grant you, according to the riches of his glory, to be strengthened with might by his Spirit in the inner man. (Ephesians 3:16)

But we have this treasure in earthen vessels, that the excellency of the power may be of God, and not of us. (2 Corinthians 4:7)

I am crucified with Christ; nevertheless I live; yet not I, but Christ liveth in me: and the life which I now live in the flesh I live by the faith of the Son of God, who loved me, and gave himself for me. (Galatians 2:20)

Let's pause just for a second and take a minute to dissect Galatians 2:20. Every second of every day, two things constantly happen. We make either much of our lives or much of Jesus. In the center of all this is us, and we choose which one to make the most of. I have been convicted about this familiar verse. When it says I am crucified, it literally means my ideas, attitude, and fleshly desires are completely annihilated, and I am fully surrendered to Jesus and His ideas, character, and desires. But what does that even look like? Well, let's just call it like it is.

When I (Angela) live,

- I make much of my desires;
- I make much of my dreams;
- I make much of those who hurt me;
- I make much of how I deserve this or that;
- I make much of those I think need to hear what I have to say;
- I make much of my opinions.

When I live, I make much of who I am and bring glory to myself, which in all honesty is a satanic characteristic, and this way of living leads to spiritual death.

When Jesus lives,

- He makes much of His truth, His Word;
- He makes much of His vision;
- He makes much of His power;
- He makes much of His love;
- He makes much of His forgiveness;
- He makes much of His grace;
- He makes much of His hope;
- He makes much of His glory.

When I die and Jesus lives through me, this way leads to life and life abundantly. When we die and let Him live, watch and see how He will use us for His glory, kingdom, and great name's sake. Isn't it supposed to be all about Jesus anyway? It's time to stop making much of us and start making much of our beloved Savior.

We cannot have that kind of power without a prayer life. Seriously, what makes us think we could ever do a pure and true work of holiness in our flesh? It won't happen. In the South, we say, "Lord, help this hot mess!" But I think we need to reword that and say, "Let's Galatians 2:20 this hot mess." We can teach a lesson based on what we know, but it won't have any power to it. The power comes only through intimate time with Jesus Christ. Jesus began His ministry by spending forty days and nights in fasting and praying, spending time with the Father (Luke 4). That is what Jesus did. Why would we think we could do it any other way? It was after this time that Jesus came in the power of the Holy Spirit. How can the Father use us if we don't spend any time with Him?

Somewhere along the way, unintentionally and gradually we moved our feet of faith away from sole dependence on the resurrected Christ, away from the Holy Spirit as our only source of power, away from desperate times of prayer and the Word.

> But we will give ourselves continually to prayer, and to the ministry of the word. (Acts 6:4)

The hope of the church has never been its cultural footing. The hope of the church has always been the resurrection power of Jesus Christ. The power of the church has never been within its measure of people but always in its measure of the Holy Spirit.

> And now I say unto you, Refrain from these men, and let them alone: for if this counsel or this work be of men, it will come to nought: but if it be of God, ye cannot overthrow it; lest haply ye be found even to fight against God. (Acts 5:38–39)

It's good to remember that there wasn't a church building for three hundred years, yet the disciples turned the world upside down for Christ. How did they do this? *They* didn't do it. They were filled with the Holy Spirit, and He did it through them. How? It's one thing to be born again, but when we die to our flesh and allow Him to completely fill every square inch of what He bought, *that* is the game-changer. Watch how He will use us for His glory.

Satan wants you powerless. He is the master of all distractions. Satan didn't tempt Jesus when He was walking on water, feeding the five thousand, or healing the sick. It was only after He had fasted and prayed. People think Satan tempted Jesus after fasting and praying because He was weak, but I don't believe Jesus was weak at all. I believe He was full of power. I think He is the perfect example of what we need to be doing. I also believe it's key to the reason why He was so angry that He flipped tables and cast out all the money changers from the temple. It's the very reason for what He is trying to speak to us. He desires for us to get to know Him, to

spend time with Him. And in doing so, we will live lives of abundance with Him. His character will ooze through our pores because we will be filled to overflowing with Him.

That's the power all of us will experience if we will just spend time with Jesus every single day, if we will just confess what needs to be confessed, because we still live in this flesh and mess up. We should make Him our focus, our priority, who we value most in our lives, whom we love and are in love with, when we feel like it and when we don't. Then we will be so filled with Jesus that we can't help but win souls. People would be drawn to us, not because of us but because of Jesus living in and through us. And here in Luke 4 is how living that powerful life starts. Spend time with Jesus, and then you will walk in the power of the Holy Spirit.

How do we fight Satan, his armies of darkness, and our own flesh? Just like Jesus did—through prayer and the Word. Again, consider this:

> But we will give ourselves continually to prayer, and to the ministry of the word. (Acts 6:4)

God can't teach us to pray if we don't show up to practice. We need to be present. Daily. Let's continue in Luke 4, with Jesus as our example. It was *after* Jesus spent time with the Father that He not only was able to fight off Satan and temptation but also went out in *power*.

> And when the devil had ended all the temptation, he departed from him for a season. And Jesus returned in the power of the Spirit into Galilee: and there went out a fame of him through all the region round about. (Luke 4:13–14)

> And they were astonished at his doctrine: for his word was with power. (Luke 4:32)

Astonish: To stun or strike dumb with sudden fear, terror, surprise, or wonder; to amaze; to confound with some sudden passion.[27]

> And they were all amazed, and spake among themselves, saying, What a word is this! for with authority and power he commandeth the unclean spirits, and they come out. (Luke 4:36)

> For God hath not given us the spirit of fear; but of power, and of love, and of a sound mind. (2 Timothy 1:7)

> But seek ye first the Kingdom of God, and his righteousness; and all these things shall be added unto you. (Matthew 6:33)

God is the God of order. Why is power first? Because of what He wants us to seek first. The kingdom of God. Seek His presence. Seek Him. When I have power, which is Jesus; when I have love, which is Jesus; and when I have a sound mind, which is Jesus, I tell you what- I have no fear. It doesn't matter what happens or what anyone ever says or threatens me with because I have Jesus. (Sidenote: You can *never* say the powerful, precious name of Jesus too much. Can I get a witness?)

> Behold, I give unto you power to tread on serpents and scorpions, and over all the power of the enemy: and nothing shall by any means hurt you. Notwithstanding in this rejoice not, that the spirits are subject unto you; but rather rejoice, because your names are written in heaven. (Luke 10:19–20)

I love what He says here. He gives you power, but He puts more emphasis on the relationship, for it is the relationship we have with Him that empowers us. He is that treasure—not what we can receive from Him but *just Him* alone. Jesus wants us to rejoice that we have a relationship with Him over the "power" He gives us. That should tell us something. That should tell us how powerful that intimate relationship truly is. It's more powerful than the power He gives us. Wow!

> After these things the word of the Lord came unto Abram in a vision, saying, Fear not, Abram: I am thy shield, and thy exceeding great reward. (Genesis 15:1)

> Now it came to pass, as they went, that he entered into a certain village: and a certain woman named Martha received him into her house. And she had a sister called Mary, which also sat at Jesus' feet, and heard his word. But Martha was cumbered about much serving, and came to him, and said, Lord, dost thou not care that my sister hath left me to serve alone? bid her therefore that she help me. And Jesus answered and said unto her, Martha, Martha, thou art careful and troubled about many things: but one thing is needful: and Mary hath chosen that good part, which shall not be taken away from her. (Luke 10:38–42)

His power is not the reward. *He* is the reward. One thing is needful, and Jesus is that one thing. When we choose other things over spending time with Him, we are literally saying, "Jesus, You are not enough for me. I don't value the cross. I don't value my relationship with You." We may not say that aloud, but that's what our actions say. Let's just call it what it is and confess it. We value *me*. We would rather watch TV than spend that time with Him. We would rather have "me time" over time with the Savior. We value doing the work of ministry over spending time with the One we claim to be serving and doing ministry for. We would rather

do the work over prayer and the Word. That truth exposes the lack of value we have for Jesus, our relationship with Him, and what He has done for us to have this relationship. Our eyes aren't fixed on Him completely. We cannot be empowered by Him if we aren't near Him. A stick of dynamite is useless without that spark of fire to ignite it. Get near the consuming fire.

> For our God is a consuming fire. (Hebrews 12:29)

> And my speech and my preaching was not with enticing words of man's wisdom, but in the demonstration of the Spirit and of power: that your faith should not stand in the wisdom of men, but in the power of God. (1 Corinthians 2:4–5)

> For the kingdom of God is not in word, but in power. (1 Corinthians 4:20)

If the kingdom of God isn't in word but in power, then wouldn't you agree that we need to be connected to that Source?

So, what is the fuel that keeps you going? I believe there are three sources we choose to abide in every moment of every day. They are the fuels of law, lust, or love. Before we look at them, let's just stop for a moment and ask the Lord to open our hearts and minds and welcome Him to show us the truth about which one is fueling us. Let's pray the following scripture together.

> Search me, O God, and know my heart: try me, and know my thoughts: and see if there be any wicked way in me, and lead me in the way everlasting. (Psalm 139:23–24)

Lord Jesus, I am in awe of You. I am astounded by Your greatness and mercies toward me. Your love is overwhelming and leaves me in wonder. I praise You for who You are. You are God. You are holy. And the reality that the holy God would want a relationship with me blows my mind. You, Jesus, simply amaze me!

Jesus, this is never an easy prayer for me to pray because it goes against my flesh and my pride. But I truly just want You, and if there is anything—anything at all—I'm allowing to be in the way of You, if there is anything or anyone I have placed before You, making him or her my idol, Lord, I am asking You to show me now. Right here, in this moment, expose it. If You aren't the Source of my life, show me. As much as it may hurt and make me uncomfortable, as much as I won't want to admit it, Father, leave no room for me to deny it. Lord, don't allow me to rush through this next part. Help me to slow down and allow Your Holy Spirit through the Word to speak to my heart and mind and clear out this temple of the things that have polluted it. I humbly bow before You at Your feet, ready to receive Your Word. In Jesus's name, I pray.

LAW

Those fueled by law live in a trap of legalism. They do the right things but have left the relationship they once had with Christ. They have strayed away from *why* they do what they do and are focused more on the work of God and not on the worship, which is the relationship.

> I know thy works, and thy labour, and thy patience, and how thou canst not bear them which are evil: and thou hast tried them which say they are apostles, and are not, and hast found them liars: And hast borne, and hast patience, and for my name's sake hast laboured, and hast not fainted. Nevertheless I have somewhat against thee, because thou hast left thy first love. Remember therefore from whence thou art fallen, and repent, and do the first works; or else I will come unto thee quickly, and will remove thy candlestick out of his place, except thou repent. (Revelation 2:2–5)

LUST

Those fueled by lust seek the recognition and praise of people. Many are involved in ministry but are doing it because they love to hear about how well they sing, teach, pray, and so forth. They are motivated by how well they work for God. They are full of pride, false humility (which is pride), and self-gratification. They like the way their words sound and are addicted to the applause of people. When we get our identity from our accomplishments and recognition, we end up in an emotional storm of vanity and our own ego, and it will *always* leave us feeling empty. If you are a child of God, your worth is found solely in Jesus Christ.

> For the time will come when they will not endure sound doctrine; but after their own lusts shall they heap to themselves teachers, having itching ears; and they shall turn away their ears from the truth, and shall be turned unto fables. (2 Timothy 4:3–4)

> (For many walk, of whom I have told you often, and now tell you even weeping, that they are the enemies of the cross of Christ: whose end is destruction, whose God is their belly, and whose glory is in their shame, who mind earthly things.) (Philippians 3:18–19)

LOVE

Those fueled by love live a life of abundance. They are filled with His Spirit and power. They seek to please Jesus and Him alone.

The thief cometh not, but for to steal, and to kill, and to destroy: I am come that they might have life, and that they might have it more abundantly. (John 10:10)

But seek ye first the kingdom of God, and his righteousness; and all these things shall be added unto you. (Matthew 6:33)

It won't be you, but it will be Jesus living through you. Seek and love Him first, and He will add everything of value to your life and enrich you with His character. When you are fueled by love, which is God, you want to live an obedient and holy life. When you are in love with someone, you will do whatever he or she wants and love what he or she loves.

Our worship is the overflow of our love for Him and reflects the relationship we have. Our praise is the overflow of our worship. Worship brings us to our knees before Him in humility, awe, and wonder. Praise brings us to our feet to shout of His greatness and majesty. Love motivates obedience and perseverance, and those who love Him will taste and see He is good and will persevere to the end, finishing strong.

Blessed is the man that endureth temptation: for when he is tried, he shall receive the crown of life, which the Lord hath promised to them that love him. (James 1:12)

Love motivates a love for others.

But love ye your enemies, and do good, and lend, hoping for nothing again; and your reward shall be great, and ye shall be the children of the Highest: for he is kind unto the unthankful and to the evil. (Luke 6:35)

For, brethren, ye have been called unto liberty; only use not liberty for an occasion to the flesh, but by love serve one another. (Galatians 5:13)

This isn't just a love for those who are outside the family of God. It is also a love for our brothers and sisters in the faith, including those of the church who have hurt us. I'm not oblivious that the enemy is all over this topic. I have had my fair share of being hurt by the church, past and present. I didn't always take these burdens to the Lord in prayer. Most of the time I allowed them to stew and build up, causing bitterness to take over my life. That never winds up being good. The only thing I know is to continually take it all to Jesus. His Word is and has always been faithful to show me how to respond in love and prayer toward the ones who hurt me, and some unfortunately hurt me deeply. I certainly haven't always been good at this, and it's definitely not my first response to pray for those who have hurt me either. But if I make Jesus my foundation, focus, and fuel, His opinion will be the only one that matters to me in any situation (Psalm 119:165).

Social media can be a bad thing. We tend to sometimes hide behind the mask of it. But posting and gossiping about other churches or other church members isn't the answer, and we know it isn't the right way to do things, especially among those who claim to be Christians. Pray for one another. Pray for your brothers and sisters, even amid hurts they have caused. Take it to Jesus and let His Word show you what to do. Family is hard. I certainly didn't always get along with my sisters. In fact, it would get downright ugly sometimes (my poor parents).

> A new commandment I give unto you, That ye love one another; as I have loved you, that ye also love one another. By this shall all men know that ye are my disciples, if ye have love one to another. (John 13:34–35)

How will the world know who Jesus is and whose we are? By loving one another as Jesus loves us. To the one who has been hurt by the church, I am deeply sorry. Please turn the other cheek, read the Word, and seek His face for guidance and comfort. To the one who continues to hurt the church, please stop. Repent and forgive those who have hurt you as well. Seek His Word to fill you with His love to fuel you.

Those fueled by love will bear the fruit of the Spirit.

> But the fruit of the Spirit is love, joy, peace, longsuffering, gentleness, goodness, faith, meekness, temperance: against such there is no law. And they that are Christ's have crucified the flesh with the affections and lusts. (Galatians 5:22–24)

God is love. That love is the power source of being able to live a life pleasing to Him. Having a relationship with Him through prayer and being in the Word plugs us into that power. What you choose to be your fuel determines who you worship. Law worships the work. Lust worships self. Love worships God. So here is the question only you can answer. Which fuel are you tapping into?

What makes someone stay faithful to following Jesus for years? What makes someone continue in the face of persecution and even death? What is it? It is the direct result of his or her passionate love for Christ alone. It isn't Jesus plus ministry. It isn't "I love Jesus and people." It isn't loving Jesus and something else. It's *just Jesus*.

In 2020, a pandemic hit the world that shook everyone to the core, yes, even born-again believers, the church. Our faith was tested and tried, and it didn't take long to find out who or what we trust in the most. The Lord taught me so much during this time. It isn't a deep or new revelation, but it is just the simple truth that you can trust God. When the world is panicking and everyone is trusting the government and media, you can trust God. When you go out in

public, when you go to church, and when you go to school, you can trust God. When chaos strikes our world, it does *not* change His plans for your life, it does *not* change His Word, and it does *not* change who our God is.

> So then faith cometh by hearing, and hearing by the word of God. (Romans 10:17)

Consistency in God's Word fuels faith. Constantly listening to the world's views fuels fear. So again, I ask, which fuel are you tapping into? We can gauge which one by our reactions to the chaos that surrounds us daily. It's so easy to get distracted by what's going on. The voice of the world is loud and at times aggressive. But the voice of truth, the Word of God, will always lead us to freedom and a peace that passes all understanding.

> Some trust in chariots, and some in horses: but we will remember the name of the Lord our God. (Psalm 20:7)

His power represents His presence. His presence represents His face. His face is what we need to be seeking. When we keep Him the number one reason why we do everything we do, He gives us the love to love others, because it is *His love*.

> When thou saidst, Seek ye my face; my heart said unto thee, Thy face, Lord, will I seek. (Psalm 27:8)

> Seek the Lord and his strength, seek his face continually. (1 Chronicles 16:11)

> Seek the Lord, and his strength: seek his face evermore. (Psalm 105:4)

> Thou has made known to me the ways of life; thou shalt make me full of joy with thy countenance. (Acts 2:28)

> Why art thou cast down, O my soul? and why art thou disquieted in me? hope thou in God: for I shall yet praise him for the help of his countenance. (Psalm 42:5)

It is all about His face, His presence. It's all about Him. May our hearts beat for Jesus. May our eyes always behold Him. May our mouths speak of only Jesus. May our hands give to and for Jesus. May our feet go with Jesus and stand upon Him. May our bodies be a living sacrifice for Jesus. May our lives be lived for Jesus. May even our deaths glorify the One who is worthy of it all, Jesus.

> I know both how to be abased, and I know how to abound: every where and in all things I am instructed both to be full and to be hungry, both to abound

and to suffer need. I can do all things through Christ which strengtheneth me. (Philippians 4:12–13)

Heavenly Father, You are all I need. You are all-powerful, the all-consuming power. Consume anything in my life that is exalting itself higher than You. I want You and You alone, not just what I can get from You, but just You. Consume me for Your glory, in Jesus's name, amen.

Beloved, you are wanted.

You are empowered.

GROUP DISCUSSION QUESTIONS

E: Empower

But we have this treasure in earthen vessels, that the excellency of the power may be of God, and not of us. (2 Corinthians 4:7)

What scriptures come to mind that prove the Lord wants to empower you to live a life devoted to Him?

_____
_____
_____
_____
_____
_____
_____

What distractions keep you from living a life of empowerment?

_____
_____
_____
_____
_____
_____
_____

Read Revelation 2:2–5 again. What is an example of a time when you were empowered by the fuel of law?

_____
_____
_____
_____
_____
_____

Read 2 Timothy 4:3–4 again. What is an example of a time when you were empowered by the fuel of lust?

_____

_____

_____

_____

_____

Read John 10:10. Those fueled by love live lives of abundance. What is an example of a time when you were empowered by the fuel of love?

_____

_____

_____

_____

_____

CHAPTER 10

WANTED
D: DELIVER

D: DELIVER

Jesus wants to *deliver* you.

He is our Deliverer.

```
Deliver: To free; to release, as from restraint; to set at liberty
one who has been in captivity.
```
[28]

Many times we go back to the old ways of doing things once we become born again. We need to come out of the mentality of "who I *was*" and boldly stand on the truth of whose we are. When we walk in this truth, it ignites a more vibrant prayer life and a stronger longing to spend time with our Savior. The enemy will try to remind us of who we were, but we can now proclaim whose we are, and we are His.

> My beloved is mine, and I am his: he feedeth among the lilies. (Song of Solomon 2:16)

> For there stood by me this night the angel of God, whose I am, and whom I serve. (Acts 27:23)

> I am my beloved's, and his desire is toward me. (Song of Solomon 7:10)

When the lies come (and they will), we can combat them with the truth. That's how we fight in this spiritual war—with the Word and prayer. We must have the mind of Christ, and the only way we can do so is to be in the Word.

> Let this mind be in you, which was also in Christ Jesus. (Philippians 2:5)

We have an enemy who wants to paralyze us with guilt and shame. Guilt and shame will keep us from moving forward. Jesus has already freed us from all that. Our past is covered in the blood, and we are no longer defined by it. We are no longer enslaved or bound by those chains. We have been delivered. We have been set free. Claim His truth about us.

> My little children, let us not love in word, neither in tongue; but in deed and in truth. And hereby we know that we are of the truth, and shall assure our hearts before him. For if our heart condemn us, God is greater than our heart, and knoweth all things. Beloved, if our heart condemn us not, then have we confidence toward God. (1 John 3:18–21)

If the enemy can get us to think wrong, he can get us to live wrong. When I believe the lies of the enemy and what the enemy says about me, I'm saying that the sacrifice Jesus paid wasn't enough to set me free, that He isn't enough to deliver me from my sin and past.

"But Angela, can Jesus really deliver me from an addiction of any kind? Can He really deliver me from depression? Can He deliver me from my reliance on others to be happy and fulfilled?"

Oh, precious one, hear this truth and let it soak into the depths of your soul. Jesus has the power to deliver your soul from an eternity in hell, to be one in heaven with Him. He has broken the power of sin, death, and the grave; and He has forgiven you of every sin, every fault, you will ever commit or think, making you new *in* Him. So, I am confident and persuaded, based on the authority and power of His Word, that yes, He can deliver you from anything and everything.

Stop here and take some time with the Savior, the conquering King, and tell Him what has you bound. What is that secret? What is the thing that keeps you up at night? What is it that the enemy taunts you with? What are the things in your life that stunt your growth in Christ?

_____

_____

_____

_____

_____

_____

_____

_____

_____

_____

_____

_____

_____

_____

_____

Everything He is we get to have. It is ours for the taking! The enemy tries to convince us that we can't have who Jesus is and what Jesus gives because of who we were. That's why we must grab hold of the truth of *whose we are.*

GOD WANTS TO DELIVER US ACCORDING TO HIS WORD

> Let my supplication come before thee: deliver me according to thy word. (Psalm 119:170)

The psalmist called on God first. "Deliver me according to thy word," which is truth. Why? Because truth makes us free. And what is truth? The Word. And who is the Word? Jesus.

> Then said Jesus to those Jews which believed on him, If ye continue in my word, then are ye my disciples indeed; and ye shall know the truth, and the truth shall make you free. (John 8:31–32)

1. God wants to deliver you from the lies that feed guilt.

> Casting down imaginations, and every high thing that exalteth itself against the knowledge of God, and bringing into captivity every thought to the obedience of Christ. (2 Corinthians 10:5)

> There is therefore now no condemnation to them which are in Christ Jesus, who walk not after the flesh, but after the Spirit. (Romans 8:1)

2. God wants to deliver us from our pasts and sins.

> Deliver me from all my transgressions: make me not the reproach of the foolish. (Psalm 39:8)

> For sin shall not have dominion over you: for ye are not under the law, but under grace. (Romans 6:14)

3. God wants to deliver us from *every* evil work.

> And the Lord shall deliver me from every evil work, and will preserve me unto his heavenly kingdom: to whom be glory for ever and ever. Amen. (2 Timothy 4:18)

4. God wants to deliver us from that great death.

> Who hath delivered us from so great a death, and doth deliver: in whom we trust that he will yet deliver us. (2 Corinthians 1:10)

5. God wants to deliver us from depression and oppression.

> Surely he shall deliver thee from the snare of the fowler, and from the noisome pestilence. (Psalm 91:3)

```
Noisome pestilence: Oppression/depression; to make one heavy.
```

> I waited patiently for the Lord; and he inclined unto me, and heard my cry. He brought me up also out of an horrible pit, out of the miry clay, and set my feet upon a rock, and established my goings. (Psalm 40:1–2)

Satan wants to keep you down within the horrible pit, the prison cell.

6. God wants to deliver us from temptation.

> The Lord knoweth how to deliver the godly out of temptations, and to reserve the unjust unto the day of judgment to be punished. (2 Peter 2:9)

> There hath no temptation taken you but such is common to man: but God is faithful, who will not suffer you to be tempted above that ye are able; but will with the temptation also make a way to escape, that ye may be able to bear it. (1 Corinthians 10:13)

7. God wants to deliver us from gripping fear.

> I sought the Lord, and he heard me, and he delivered me from all my fears. (Psalm 34:4)

> But whoso hearkeneth unto me shall dwell safely, and shall be quiet from fear of evil. (Proverbs 1:33)

8. God wants to deliver us from difficult situations.

> My God hath sent his angel, and hath shut the lions' mouths, that they have not hurt me. (Daniel 6:22)

> The angel of the Lord encampeth round about them that fear him, and delivereth them. (Psalm 34:7)

God allowed him to be in that difficult situation so He could shut the mouths of lions, so others could see the power of the God of Daniel.

9. God wants to deliver us from resentment and bitterness.

We can easily become bitter and resentful when trouble comes, but look at Stephen's reaction in Acts 7.

> And they stoned Stephen, calling upon God, and saying, Lord Jesus, receive my spirit. And he kneeled down, and cried with a loud voice, Lord, lay not this sin to their charge. And when he had said this, he fell asleep. (Acts 7:59–60)

> And call upon me in the day of trouble: I will deliver thee, and thou shalt glorify me. (Psalm 50:15)

Do you need deliverance in your marriage? From a difficult situation? From a sin? He is your Deliverer.

MEN AND WOMEN IN THE BIBLE GOD DELIVERED

- Moses, the man of patience (Numbers 20:8–12)
- Abraham, the man of faith (Genesis 22:1–14)
- Noah, the man of endurance (Genesis 6)
- Elijah, the man of boldness (1 Kings 18:20–40)
- Daniel, the man of devotion (Daniel 1:8–16)
- David, the man after God's own heart (1 Samuel 17, 24)
- Job, the man of perseverance (Job 1:13–23)
- Shadrach, Meshach, and Abednego—the underdogs (Daniel 3)
- Paul, the missionary and the man against all odds (Acts 9, 22)
- Hannah, the woman of great faith and obedience (1 Samuel 1:28)
- Abigail, the woman of commitment (1 Samuel 25)
- Esther, the woman of bravery and courage (Esther 1–8)

Turn in your Bible to 2 Samuel 22:1–51 and read it aloud. Every bit of what God gave to David is yours too. These men and women of the Bible were average people just like you and me. All that was available to these characters in the Bible are the same things that are available to us. We tend to romanticize the characters in the Bible, thinking, *God can do that, yes! But would He do that for me?* Yes, He will.

> Forasmuch then as the children are partakers of flesh and blood, he also himself likewise took part of the same; that through death he might destroy him that had the power of death, that is, the devil; and deliver them who through fear of death were all their lifetime subject to bondage. For verily he took not on

him the nature of angels; but he took on him the seed of Abraham. Wherefore in all things it behoved him to be made like unto his brethren, that he might be a merciful and faithful high priest in things pertaining to God, to make reconciliation for the sins of the people. For in that he himself hath suffered being tempted, he is able to succour them that are tempted. (Hebrews 2:14–18)

God hasn't changed. Everything God was in the Old Testament and New Testament is the same today. It hasn't been watered down, tainted, or discontinued. It's still available to us right now.

He delivered me from my strong enemy, and from them which hated me: for they were too strong for me. (Psalm 18:17)

I sought the Lord, and he heard me, and delivered me from all my fears. (Psalm 34:4)

For thou hast delivered my soul from death: wilt not thou deliver my feet from falling, that I may walk before God in the light of the living? (Psalm 56:13)

He wants to deliver us from *everything*.

Let me introduce you to my friend and sister in Christ, Shawn Hager. Shawn participated in our *Wanted* home Bible study. I will never forget what happened during those lessons but especially what happened in Shawn. I have asked her to share her experience and the testimony of her deliverance and freedom in Jesus.

In early December 2020, my precious sister, Angela, started a Bible study with six other women. It was a study called *Wanted*. Ever heard of it? I honestly thought it would be like every other Bible study I have been to, with sound truth and some deep conversations to chew on throughout the week. I had no idea the Lord was about to radically shake, expose, and change my life.

The temple lesson shook me to the depths of my soul. I was the Christian who really didn't put much value into my body being the temple of the Holy Ghost, let alone the cost Jesus paid for me to have this honor and privilege. When we read about Jesus casting out the money changers and flipping tables because they had made the house of God a den of thieves, the Holy Spirit spoke so loudly to my heart. "Shawn, you have polluted and continue to pollute My temple with your secrets and lies." I still tremble as I remember that moment.

2020 was a challenging year, to say the least. But my year started off with a suicide attempt in February. I have been saved since 2005, but every time I tried to stand up, I fell. Every time I advanced, I was pushed back. Every time I stepped up into ministry, I retreated just as fast. Nothing I built stood. I knew I was saved. I knew I would go to heaven when I died, but I couldn't, for the life of me, figure out why my life was full of confusion, chaos, and ultimately severe depression.

After a five-day stay in a mental hospital, I began throwing myself into counseling and a Christ-centered recovery program, where I exposed a temptation I had secretly struggled with: homosexuality. I worked the steps and was honest in my struggles, but the temptation of that never lightened up. When I thought I had found the root cause of *why* I was gay, it still never went away, even though I hadn't had a relationship for many years.

It was in the "W: Living Water" lesson when the Holy Spirit exposed the problem. And I will be honest; I wasn't ready for it, not at all. I don't have the freedom to tell you about the exposure simply because others are involved who aren't comfortable with me sharing it. Nonetheless, it was a very painful and scary moment of revelation of what was lying beneath the hard soil of my heart. Jesus was never condemning, but the exposure was absolutely uncomfortable and sickening.

"A: Adorn" brought a whole other issue to the surface. I was still holding onto the label "gay Christian," and the Holy Spirit basically told me that cannot be. It angered me. Why couldn't I just have this? I had already given up the lifestyle many years back. But as I began to understand what exactly the robe of righteousness was and how I was treating it by choosing to keep my label, suddenly being a gay Christian didn't have the "self-sacrificing" tone I thought it did. It actually began to sound more prideful and self-centered than anything. The "N: Nurture" lesson asked a question: "What is stunting your growth?" There was no more denying it to myself anymore, and I wrote down the truth in my book. "Same Sex Attraction on a daily basis and my inability to let go of that identity." By the time we got to "E: Empower," the intensity of the war raging inside me was more than I could take. I knew the Lord had forgiven me, but James 5:16 says, "Confess your faults one to another, and pray one for another, that ye may be healed. The effectual fervent prayer of a righteous man availeth much." What Jesus had exposed back in "W" needed to be confessed

to another. And bless Angela's heart, she was the one who heard my confession that day after class. It was one of the most difficult things I have ever done in my life but one of the most rewarding. Here's why.

That was the thing that was polluting this temple. It was blocking the doors, keeping me from being able to get rid of everything else. It was that one thing that kept my head hung low, and once that weight was removed, I was able to lift my head, and for the first time in my life, I was able to see the face of Jesus. I haven't been the same since.

From that afternoon forward, things in my life began to rapidly change for the better. I was no longer asking and begging God to fix things or change me. I was longing just to get to *know* Him. I wanted to be in the Word as much as possible. I surrounded myself with a few others who loved to talk about Jesus and didn't look at me like I had four heads and a mustache when I shared how He was moving in my life. Jesus became so personal and real to me as our relationship began to grow deep and intimate. However, there was still one issue that remained. I had yet to let go of the "gay Christian" label. Why? Because I didn't know a life without being gay and feared what it would be like without it. As wrong and twisted as that sounds, and as much as it left me lacking and living in the "less than," I was terrified to let it go.

The Lord has perfect timing. In June 2021 at a ladies' retreat, the Lord brought me to a defining moment. Jesus used Dawn Mason, a dear friend of mine, the speaker at the event, to simply ask me, "Do you want to be made well?" It wasn't until I was driving home that night, pulling over at a creepy gas station at 1 a.m., that I finally answered His question, with much fear and trembling. "Yes."

Nothing magical happened. It wasn't until a few days later, when I had an impure thought about a woman, that for the first time in my life, it turned my stomach. And, honey, I have been walking in His freedom from homosexuality ever since. Notice I said, "His freedom." I tried everything I knew to rid myself of this torment of struggling with homosexuality and being a born-again believer. I prayed, rejected pursuing that lifestyle, read my Bible, went to church, was involved with different ministries, and went on mission trips; I did all the right things. But when I stopped looking at the madness and looked up into the face of Jesus, that's when things began to shift. When I stopped looking for Him to give me something and I started looking for Him alone, everything changed.

Jesus. He didn't give me freedom. He *is* freedom. The more and more I know Him, everything He is becomes part of me. Love. Joy. Peace. Hope. Patience. When hard things come, I'm not rattled like I used to be. When the Lord exposes other things that are polluting His temple within me, I am quicker to respond. It isn't easy. Some have been heartbreaking and painful, but I have found I am addicted to surrender because the more I surrender, the closer Jesus and I become. I am telling you, there is no other place I would rather be. Jesus is worth it all and worthy of my all. Just give me Jesus.

What does it mean when we say, "Give me Jesus"? Because it isn't a cute phrase to print on a T-shirt or sign a card with. No, ma'am! When we say, "Give me Jesus," we are saying, "Give me life, truth, love, hope, peace, joy, freedom, power, water, bread, righteousness, and wisdom." All these things are who Jesus is! "Give me Jesus" is a plea for more of Him, not for what He can do or give me. It isn't enough for me to want to be saved. I want the Savior. I want the Giver more than the gifts, the Healer more than the healing, the Provider more than the provision. I just want Jesus!

Open your Bible and flip over to Esther 4:1–16. How does this story make you feel? What truths pop off the pages? I don't know what all is going on in your life; nor do I know what the Lord is bringing you through, but you have been born for such a time as this. *This is the moment.* It's not time to panic; it's time to pray. It's not time to retreat; it's time to push forward. It's not time to shut up. It's time to speak up. It's not time to hide. It's time to shine. It's not time to fear; it's time to have faith.

Rise up, Esther. He is using you for this time, this moment. Be bold. Be brave. Speak out for this is what you have been created for. You can make a difference in this world for Jesus Christ. Someone somewhere is depending on you to rise and do what God has called you to do. Don't be influenced by an ever-changing world but be influenced by God's never-changing Word. This world is trying to conform us to its way of thinking, and it will take supernatural courage to be different and stand up against it.

Remember, though, that you are in good company. Joseph was sold into slavery for being different. Daniel was thrown into a den of lions for being different. Jesus was nailed to the cross for being different. And there is a whole list of others in Hebrews 11 who are in the cloud of witnesses the Bible talks about in Hebrews 12:1. That is the company that went before you, and you will stand among them when you choose Jesus above everything and everyone. Take your place, Esther. Take your place.

Then said Jesus to those Jews which believed on him, If ye continue in my word, then are ye my disciples indeed; and ye shall know the truth and the truth shall make you free. (John 8:31–32)

Lord Jesus, I am so thankful You are the truth. I am overwhelmed by the reality that I get to *know You*! I am full of praise that *You* are *everything* I could ever want or need. It is You my heart has always been longing for. It is You who has satisfied my soul, giving purpose and reason to my life, and You are what I want. I am *wanted* by You, and now You are all I want.

Thank You for Your freedom. Thank You for this abundant life that is far beyond what I could have dreamed of. Thank You for delivering me from everything in my life. Even if I don't "feel" it or don't see it, Lord, I believe Your Word. I believe You over my emotions and situations. Because You cannot lie and You never change, I place my soul, my life, and my faith completely and solely *in You*. There are no words to say that can explain the magnitude of my thankfulness to You. So here is my life. Take it all. Help me to abide in You for You and Your glory! In Jesus's name.

Beloved, you are wanted.

You are delivered.

You are His.

GROUP DISCUSSION QUESTIONS

D: Deliver

Let my supplication come before thee: deliver me according to thy word. (Psalm 119:170)

What has Jesus delivered you from through the course of getting to know Him? What scriptures has He used to help you?

_____

_____

_____

_____

_____

_____

_____

What are some of the old ways you are still going back to? What is the secret that keeps you up at night? What scriptures can you use to combat what is listed?

_____

_____

_____

_____

_____

_____

_____

What comes to mind when you read 2 Samuel 22:1–51?

_____

_____

_____

_____

_____

_____

Do you *truly* believe God wants to deliver *you* from whatever you are bound to? Why or why not?

_____

_____

_____

_____

_____

_____

If the Lord has delivered you, are you telling others about the event? About Him? Why or why not?

_____

_____

_____

_____

_____

_____

CHAPTER 11

SO, NOW WHAT?

Did you go to church camp as a kid or teenager? For me it was a long weekend of powerful sermons, challenging devotions, and group-building games. We committed our thoughts and lives to the Lord, promised to hold one another accountable to the decisions made, and we came home all fired up about what the Lord had done while we were at church camp. But then Monday came. The same struggles, peer pressures, and daily stresses were still there, and that emotional high we had felt was now nothing but a smoldering ember.

As the Lord poured into me the truths of *Wanted*, I had a similar experience after the "D: Deliver" lesson. There was such a fiery, passionate zeal burning within me that I didn't want it to ever end. I didn't want it to become like it was in the days and weeks after a "church camp." You know, where the white-hot flame would slowly burn out. That was when the Lord asked me whether what happened was based off an emotion or the Word? Was I relying on how I felt? Or on truth? There is a choice that will be made moment by moment, breath by breath for the rest of our days here on earth. Why? Because we wrestle between Spirit and our flesh.

> This I say then, Walk in the Spirit, and ye shall not fulfil the lust of the flesh. For the flesh lusteth against the Spirit, and the Spirit against the flesh: and these are contrary the one to the other: so that ye cannot do the things that ye would. (Galatians 5:16–17)

But Angela, what does that look like? I'm glad you asked that question because I asked the Lord the same thing, and here is the answer He gave me from His Word.

> Know ye not that your bodies are the members of Christ? shall I then take the members of Christ, and make them the members of an harlot? God forbid. What? know ye not that he which is joined to an harlot is one body? for two, saith he, shall be one flesh. But he that is joined unto the Lord is one spirit. Flee fornication. Every sin that a man doeth is without the body; but he that committeth fornication sinneth against his own body. What? know ye not that your body is the temple of the Holy Ghost which is in you, which ye have of God, and ye are not your own? For ye are bought with a price: therefore glorify God in your body, and in your spirit, which are God's. (1 Corinthians 6:15–20)

Words matter in scripture. God is so vast and perfect; therefore, so is His Word because He is the Word. There is a divine purpose to the words He chooses and how He intricately places them throughout His Holy Scriptures.

I knew before I began to study just a small portion of the temple that it would engulf me. I knew that all He showed me would be so overwhelming, and it has been. But the beauty of it all is that through this, I have been able to know Jesus more deeply than I did before. He

has allowed me to see His heart for His bride. His love is so overwhelming for us that I can't find the human words to express it. But He has also opened my eyes to the condition of the church and my own self with its idols, which has broken my heart and given me anguish unlike anything I have ever had before.

Jesus is mercy. He is love. He is grace. He is salvation and beauty. He is breathtaking. He is sovereign. He is our Judge, and He is truth. It isn't enough to just have parts of Him. We must have all of Him. It is because of His mercy that He exposes the sins that corrupt us. It is because of this indescribable pure love for us that He cuts us open with His truth, the Word, exposing darkness to His light. This allows us to be consumed with His refining fire, which will burn away all that isn't of Him—that is, if we choose Him.

Saying yes to Jesus and no to my flesh isn't easy. It's painful and difficult. There is a real battle that rages within each of us. But as difficult as it may be, I'm embracing the all-consuming Fire. I am embracing the Truth. I am embracing the Hammer. I am embracing the Sword. I am embracing the Refiner. I am embracing Jesus Christ because He is all these and so much more.

We are not our own. We were bought with a price. These aren't just some churchy words we say on a Sunday; they come from the Word. But do we truly believe what He says of us? Of me? Does He not deserve our full devotion? As I read the verses above, I had to ask myself, *Am I a devoted bride or a distracted harlot?* See, even though Jesus has delivered us, we are still in a fight against our flesh and its wants and desires. As the Lord continues to make His bride ready for His return, as He continues to expose what is polluting His temple, our bodies, we will always be faced with a choice: Jesus or another? Am I a bride or a harlot?

> And this I speak for your own profit; not that I may cast a snare upon you, but for that which is comely, and that ye may attend upon the Lord without distraction. (1 Corinthians 7:35)

Attend: To go with or accompany as a companion, minister, or servant. To be present; to accompany or be united to. To await: to remain, abide.[29]

Once you are born again and sealed with the Holy Spirit, Satan cannot steal your soul. So he will do everything he can to keep you from desiring to "attend upon the Lord." His goal is to take your eyes off Jesus and keep you from looking like our Savior, so he will send weapons of mass distraction. In Luke 10, Martha is "cumbered about much serving" (Luke 10:40). and Jesus called her out on it.

Martha, Martha, thou art careful and troubled about many things. (Luke 10:41)

Satan will do everything he can to distract us from the pursuit of God, our personal time with the Father, and worship with one another as the body of Christ, even if the distraction is service and ministry. But here is the thing: *there is no demon or spirit of distraction.* Don't miss that. We blame our lack of time and devotion on our distractions, as if they have some type of supernatural hold over us. The painful truth is that it's *my choice* to be distracted. I choose whether to be distracted by these weapons, whatever they may be and whatever form they come in.

In Luke 4, Jesus was presented with three distractions: the lust of the flesh, the lust of the eyes, and the pride of life. And Jesus chose not to be distracted by any of them; rather, He chose to be obedient to the scriptures and used them to fight against these distractions.

> But I fear, lest by any means, as the serpent beguiled Eve through his subtilty, so your minds should be corrupted from the simplicity that is in Christ. (2 Corinthians 11:3)

Beguile: To elude by craft. To elude any thing disagreeable by amusement or other means; to beguile the tedious day with sleep.[30]

Satan doesn't use any new tactics or schemes. The same weapons he used against Eve in the Garden of Eden are the same ones he used against our Lord and Savior in the wilderness, and they are the very same ones he uses against us today. In my flesh, I don't want to pray or be at His feet. Remember, there are two enemies at work against the born-again believer in Jesus Christ: Satan with his army and our own flesh. Prayer and the ministry of the Word aren't things that come from the natural world. They are supernatural. But if I truly want to "attend upon the Lord," praying and sitting at the feet of Jesus *must be* more than just checking a box. I may look like a Mary on the outside but have a Martha mind. I may physically be in my prayer closet with my Bible open; my eyes may read the words, and I may even say them aloud, but my mind could be somewhere else, thinking about anything else. We beg Him for His presence, but when was the last time we gave Him *our* presence? Our full attention?

Look at the definition of *beguiled* again. There was a word in there I wasn't expecting, nor did I like. It is *sleep.* How many times do we hit the snooze button or roll over when the Lord is waking us up to spend time with Him? I know I do. By doing so, we are stating, with our choice to roll over, that time with Him isn't valuable to us. Spending time with Him so He can speak to us and give us the strength, encouragement, and nourishment we need isn't a priority. We lean on our own understanding and believe sleep is what is needed for the day ahead, not reading the Word of God and spending time with Him at His feet. I find it no coincidence that the Word tells us to wake up.

Wherefore he saith, Awake thou that sleepest, and arise from the dead, and Christ shall give thee light. (Ephesians 5:14)

And that, knowing the time, that now it is high time to awake out of sleep: for now is our salvation nearer than when we believed. (Romans 13:11)

In 1 Corinthians 6, the Holy Spirit could have used "disobedient children" or "enemy of God" when painting a picture of what idols look like in us, but He didn't. He used a very specific word. He said "harlot." And He could have used the blanket word of *sin,* but He said "fornication." If we aren't walking in the obedience of the Word as a bride, then we are walking in the disobedience of the Word as a harlot. There is no middle ground. It is black and white. He is intentional, and words matter. So what does He want me to do with my body, which is the house of the Holy Spirit?

Turn to Mark 11:15–17 in your Bible.

Jesus didn't say His house would be called a house of preaching or a house of ministry. No! Jesus said His house, His bride, His body would be called a house of prayer.

Even them will I bring to my holy mountain, and make them joyful in my house of prayer: their burnt-offerings and their sacrifices shall be accepted upon mine altar; for mine house shall be called an house of prayer for all people. (Isaiah 56:7)

Oh my dove, that are in the clefts of the rock, in the secret places of the stairs, let me see thy countenance, let me hear thy voice; for sweet is thy voice, and thy countenance is comely. (Song of Solomon 2:14)

A house of prayer represents a relationship with God the Father. God *wants* you! He delights in seeing you and hearing your voice in the secret place (prayer and the Word).

He desires an intimate relationship with us, yet we read a verse or passage, say a quick prayer, check a box, and think nothing more about Him the rest of the day. I know that's what we do because I have done it myself. We make time for what we value. We make time for what we honor. We make time for what we are in love with. We not only make time for it, but we want to make the most of that time and make it beautiful. We want to pour ourselves fully into it.

Blessed be the Lord God of our fathers, which hath put such a thing as this in the king's heart, to beautify the house of the Lord which is in Jerusalem. (Ezra 7:27)

To beautify the house of God is a purposeful, diligent, daily choice to choose what Jesus finds valuable. We honor Him by taking out the things in our lives that pollute His temple. I'm not talking about cutting carbs and only drinking water, but it's removing the thoughts that aren't pleasing to Him. It's removing the selfish intents behind the things we do. If the intent is for us to be seen, heard, recognized, or *thanked* because we were there, that is false humility, which is pride. God hates pride, and pride pollutes the sanctuary of God.

Let this mind be in you, which was also in Christ Jesus. (Philippians 2:5)

Then all the people went to the house of Baal, and brake it down, and brake his altars and his images in pieces, and slew Mattan the priest of Baal before the altars. Also Jehoiada appointed the offices of the house of the Lord by the hand of the priests the Levites, whom David had distributed in the house of the Lord, to offer the burnt-offerings of the Lord, as it is written in the law of Moses, with rejoicing and with singing, as it was ordained by David. And he set the porters at the gates of the house of the Lord, that none which was unclean in any thing should enter in. (2 Chronicles 23:17–19)

Those who worship Him must do so in Spirit and in truth (John 4:24), prayer, and the Word (Acts 6:4). That is why we pray the Word. When we place anything, anything at all, above Him, that becomes an idol, and we replace the furnishings (the altar, laver, candlestick, shewbread, altar of incense, and mercy seat) with TV, sleep, religion, and Netflix. The greatest way to answer what we value the most is to ask ourselves where we spend most of our time. And the older we get, we discover time is certainly more valuable these days, isn't it? We get all excited about the next season of our favorite shows and are willing to spend ten hours binge-watching it and think nothing of it. We will move our schedules around to make sure we have time to fit it into our lives. But when was the last time we spent ten hours on our faces at the feet of Jesus?

Remember those nights when we would stay up all night with the devil, partying and hanging out with friends? When was the last time we stayed up all night with Jesus in His Word, getting to know Him and allowing His Word to wash over us and transform our minds and break our hearts for what breaks His? Staying up all night with Jesus will rock your world. It will change your life. That person you were when the sun went down won't be the same person when the sun comes up. Even in our own thoughts, if there is anything we place higher than Jesus in what we think, dwell on, meditate on, and so forth, we have become a thief. A harlot.

Harlot: A woman who prostitutes her body for hire, one who forsakes her God and worships idols.[31]

When we put any thing or people before the King of kings and the Lord of lords, our Savior, our Jesus, they are not only idols we worship but also lovers with whom we are cheating on Him. And not only that, but because the Holy Spirit of God dwells within us, we not only cheat on Him but do so when He is in the house. Lord, forgive us.

> And he brought me into the inner court of the Lord's house, and, behold, at the door of the temple of the Lord, between the porch and the altar, were about five and twenty men, with their backs toward the temple of the Lord, and their faces toward the east; and they worshipped the sun toward the east. Then he said unto me, Hast thou seen this, O son of man? Is it a light thing to the house of Judah that they commit the abominations which they commit here? for they have filled the land with violence, and have returned to provoke me to anger: and, lo, they put the branch to their nose. (Ezekiel 8:16–17)

This chapter of Ezekiel is about the Lord exposing to the prophet Ezekiel what was taking place in secret *within* the temple of the Lord. Each new exposure was worse than the one before it. The words at the end of verse 17 that talk about a branch being put to their noses caught my attention and caused me to dig a little deeper into what was truly happening. So, let's walk through this together.

First, the twenty-five men had their backs to the temple. They literally turned their backs on the presence and glory of God. Not only did they turn their backs on the Almighty, but they worshipped the sun. I looked up historical rituals of how the sun god was worshipped and was surprised to see that placing a branch before one's nose isn't a descriptive phrase; it was a literal part of this type of worship in Persia. It is said that sun worshippers held a branch from a tamarisk, a Homa tree, or a bunch of dates or pomegranates over their noses and mouths so their breath might not contaminate the glory of the rising deity. It was a continual mocking of God and against God from *within the temple*. They were worshipping creation and not the Creator in *His temple*.

So, what does any of this have to do with us? Everything. It's another example in the Word of God of man choosing other things to worship, to obey, instead of the Lord. He calls us to meet with Him in the morning, and we turn our backs and worship something else. Just like the twenty-five men who turned their backs in the inner court of the Lord (in the temple) and faced the sun to worship it, placing something before their faces to avoid contaminating them, we do the very same thing. We roll over, and the branches we put before our faces are our phones. We turn to social media, email, texts, friends, and family; and we make them our priority. We seek them first in the morning, not God. Lord, forgive us.

We have multiple lovers because Jesus just isn't enough for us anymore. We choose our understandings and agendas, even our ways of doing church with our man-made traditions and religions over Him. We have left our First Love and worship ourselves, not the Lord.

The thought crossed my mind a time or two regarding the reason Jesus was so passionately angry in the temple in Mark 11. Jesus is holy; He is perfect and righteous. But Jesus is also a very jealous God. We don't talk about it very much because it makes us uncomfortable to think of God as jealous. But I also believe it makes us uncomfortable because the truth of this brings conviction to our hearts, minds, and souls. It shines a spotlight on the fact that we are turning to other things and/or people to satisfy us rather than to the *only One* who can, Jesus Christ.

Have you ever been cheated on? Can you for a second imagine walking into your house and catching your spouse in the very act of adultery? What would that do to you? How would it affect you? How would it break your heart? There is an indescribable pit in your stomach of betrayal and hurt that not only makes you want to throw up, but an anger wells up from deep within. I can imagine why Christ must have been so passionately angry when He saw that His temple was filled with everything except Him. We should have no other gods before Him. No other idols. No other lovers. And when He walked in and saw what His temple had become, what was allowed to take place, it was as if a husband had caught his wife in the very act of adultery. Oh, to think how I have broken His heart with the things I have allowed in my life, that I have chosen to put in His place, and what I have devoted my time and energy to other than Jesus, the Lover of my soul.

I could write out the scriptures here, but I want you to see them on the pages of your Bible for yourself. Turn to Jeremiah 7:8–14. This passage comes alive, and I can feel and hear Him speaking as a Husband who has been cheated on. Here are some other passages that convey the same betrayal our Lord was feeling then, and I believe is experiencing now when He looks at His Bride, the Church.

> Woe is me for my hurt! my wound is grievous: but I said, Truly this is a grief, and I must bear it. My tabernacle is spoiled, and all my cords are broken: my children are gone forth of me, and they are not: there is none to stretch forth my tent any more, and to set up my curtains. (Jeremiah 10:19–20)

> My face will I turn also from them, and they shall pollute my secret place: for the robbers shall enter into it, and defile it. (Ezekiel 7:22)

> Is it not written, My house shall be called of all nations the house of prayer? but ye have made it a den of thieves. (Mark 11:17)

Jesus is the Bridegroom, and we are the bride. It has always been all about a relationship with Him. Jesus came to make things right, to restore what was lost, and that was the personal, real, intimate fellowship of God with us. It's about going back to our First Love. It's about going back to why we do the things we do. Why do we show up on Sundays? Why do we serve in ministry? Why do we go on mission trips? What are the motives behind doing and serving in the things we do? The service should be birthed out of a passionate love for our Bridegroom, our Savior, our Lord Jesus. Any other reason pollutes and defiles this temple, which He bought, making us adulterous harlots.

> Now he which stablisheth us with you in Christ, and hath anointed us, is God; who hath also sealed us, and given the earnest of the Spirit in our hearts. (2 Corinthians 1:21–22)

We are the temple of the Holy Spirit, and He is the seal, the earnest, Jesus sent as a promise that He will come back for His bride. If it's important to God, it should be important to us. He betrothed us to Himself. Like it has been mentioned before, the Holy Spirit is much better than any two-karat diamond ring (1 Corinthians 3:16–17, 23).

I read the Old Testament stories of how the glory of God filled Solomon's temple. His glory was so magnificent and powerful that the priests, those God had anointed and appointed to do His ministry within the temple, couldn't even stand, let alone speak. That same glory spoken of is the very same glory that now fills our bodies. We were made for more. Despite all the fornication and adultery we have committed and the idols we have set up in our houses, all we have to do is repent. Turn around back to Jesus, back to our First Love. Tear down what we have chosen to place before Him. Forsaking whatever the *thing* is and laying aside the weight of sin that so easily besets us (Hebrews 12:1–2), we can run back to Jesus.

Look to Jesus. Come back to Him. Even how we serve can be done in our flesh, which is pride, and we have made ourselves idols. All that's needed is to "Galatians 2:20 this hot mess," come back, and fall in love with Jesus. He even gives us His perfect, untainted, pure love by which to love Him back with. He does all of it for us. We just need to choose Him and allow Him to expose the things in our lives that are not of Him. He rebukes those He loves, not because He wants us to miss out on anything. No. He bled and died so we might have life and have it more abundantly. This isn't to take away but to give us more. More of Him. He is life. He is joy. He is love. He is peace. He is hope. He is strength and courage. He is everything, and He is enough. We don't need to work our way back to Him; all we have to do is fall back in love with Him and choose Him over the distractions that have crept into our houses, which we have allowed to become our lovers. And when we choose to look back at Jesus, He is so captivating and beautiful to behold that we will *want* to surrender it all, our all, to Him because

He is worthy of it all. We will want to continuously choose the good part, just as Mary did, by sitting at His feet daily. And when we do, it won't be taken away from us. God is keeping good books, not just with our tithe but with our time.

> Entertainment is the devil's substitute for joy. The more joy you
> have in the Lord, the less entertainment you need.
> —Leonard Ravenhill

The more I seek His face through the Word, which is a reflection of His face as if looking in a dim mirror, the more I know Him. And one day soon, that sky is going to split open, and the bride of Christ will meet her Bridegroom in the air, and we will behold His literal face, and it will be worth it all.

Entertainment pollutes yearning for spiritual growth. Two things are needed to break the cycle and the strongholds all these distractions have on us: prayer and the Word (Acts 6:4). You cannot have one without the other. They go hand in hand.

> O God, my heart is fixed; I will sing and give praise, even with my glory. (Psalm 108:1)

The heart cannot taste what the eyes haven't seen. Eyes on Jesus!

> When thou saidst, Seek ye my face; my heart said unto thee, Thy face, Lord, will I seek. (Psalm 27:8)

> For a day in thy courts is better than a thousand. I had rather be a doorkeeper in the house of my God, than to dwell in the tents of wickedness. (Psalm 84:10)

Our God is worthy to be sought. I would rather dwell in the doorframe of the house of my God than live and dwell in the grandest house this world could offer me.

> But he answered and said, It is not meet to take the children's bread, and cast it to dogs. And she said, Truth, Lord: yet the dogs eat of the crumbs which fall from their masters' table. (Matthew 15:26–27)

Jesus Christ is still our Master. I would choose to eat the crumbs from the Master's table because where are the crumbs? They are at His feet. I just want to be at His feet, where the good part is, where what Jesus said is needful and what won't be taken away. Intimate, sweet fellowship with my Savior, my Champion, my Beloved … that is all I want. Do you?

Turn with me in your Bible to Ezra 3:6–13. Look at how the Word describes the reaction to just the foundation of the temple being laid after the enemy destroyed it. I can't imagine

what these ancient men were thinking when the foundation was laid. The Bible says they were weeping because they remembered what the first temple was like and how important it was to them. They had been there. They had experienced it. I believe they were weeping not only because what had been lost was now being rebuilt but because now their children would get to experience this holy and sacred place. Their children and their children would now experience the presence, glory, majesty, and power of the almighty, holy God.

If you read the next few chapters in Ezra, you will see that an enemy revolted against those rebuilding it. All throughout the Old Testament, there was always a resistance against building the temple. Over and over again, the people needed to continuously tear down idols, high places, and groves; war against the enemies who would steal the vessels out of the house of the Lord and then reclaim them; and rebuild the temple. These aren't historical events that took place just to give us background, but they are examples of what we need to do because *we* are now the house of the Lord. He is still calling us to remove our idols, tear down our high places and groves, war against the enemy of our carnality, take back what the enemy has stolen from us, and rebuild.

Do you ever wonder why this even matters? Satan knew then (and he still knows now) that if we, the children of God, grasped the importance and value God placed on the Old Testament temple and the truth that we are now *that* temple and that His Holy Spirit dwells in us, it would radically change our lives. If we truly believe what the Bible says about the glory of God now residing in our bodies, that we have been bought with a price to have a personal relationship with the Father, there would be no power in hell that could ever stop us from living lives fully surrendered to God. If Satan keeps us from knowing this truth, he keeps us from living powerful, abundant lives. We live in the "less than" of what we are, the temple of God.

Unfortunately, this will be an ongoing situation until Jesus calls us home or that trumpet blows. Just because He has done a great work in you through this *Wanted* Bible study doesn't mean the war and work are over. He will continue to beautify His temple (that's you) until you take your last breath in this life and take your first in glory. This also means you will be at war with the enemy and your flesh, constantly having to choose what you value most. If we valued Jesus and whose we are, we would be ready to tear down, ready to war with the enemy to take back what he has stolen, ready to rebuild the waste places and the breaches; and we would be ready to watch and pray, always. It's about Jesus. It has always been and will always be about Jesus forever and ever and ever.

Read 2 Chronicles 23:17–19.

This is the mind we need to have. I know I'm reading a lot from the Old Testament, but guess what? Jesus is the Beginning and the End; this Word is the Alpha and Omega,

and everything in between is still Him. It all goes together. These things still matter to God today. The Old Testament may not be written to me in this age, but it's still profitable for doctrine, reproof, and correction. And it's also a word that will cut me open and expose everything within me that is not of God, that I need to tear down and get rid of. That is what God's Word does. He is a good God, and He wants us to be holy because He is holy. That's our motive. That's what should be in and on our hearts, the mindset that I won't let *anything* come into my life, into this temple, my body, that dishonors the Lord. I will set no evil thing before my eyes.

Now look at 2 Chronicles 24:4–5, 13; 25:2.

I think we start off well, but if we don't stay faithful in prayer and in the Word, we end up doing things like they did in 2 Chronicles 25:2. We can lead and do all the right things in the flesh, but they won't mean anything. They will all be in vain, and they will all be burned.

> Are ye so foolish? having begun in the Spirit, are ye now made perfect by the flesh? (Galatians 3:3)

> I beseech you therefore, brethren, by the mercies of God, that ye present your bodies a living sacrifice, holy, acceptable unto God, which is your reasonable service. And be not conformed to this world: but be ye transformed by the renewing of your mind, that ye may prove what is that good, and acceptable, and perfect, will of God. (Romans 12:1–2)

The only way we can have that perfect heart before God is if we continually come before Him and allow His Word to wash us and cleanse our hearts of all impurities that would or could taint the work of the Holy Spirit. We need to allow His Word to prune and strip away everything that is of this world and flesh we are still holding onto. Seriously, what makes us think we could ever do a pure and true work of holiness in our wicked, evil flesh? A divine work that comes from heaven must come from the Word, Jesus. And the only way that will happen is if we die and allow His Word to dwell in us richly.

> I am crucified with Christ: nevertheless I live; yet not I, but Christ liveth in me: and the life which I now live in the flesh I live by the faith of the Son of God, who loved me, and gave himself for me. (Galatians 2:20)

> Let the word of Christ dwell in you richly in all wisdom; teaching and admonishing one another in psalms and hymns and spiritual songs, singing with grace in your hearts to the Lord. (Colossians 3:16)

We have no business being on any platform, doing any type of ministry, if we haven't been alone with Jesus at His feet. If we choose to be at His feet, He will begin to fill every square footage of this house, our bodies; and just like the disciples in Acts who turned the world upside down, He will do the same through us. But again, it is our choice, and what we choose reveals what we find valuable.

> ...but be filled with the Spirit; speaking to yourselves in psalms and hymns and spiritual songs, singing and making melody in your heart to the Lord. (Ephesians 5:18-19)

What happens first is that I am *filled* with Him, and *then* I am speaking. Then I get to sing. Then I get to preach. Then I get to serve. Then I get to pray. Then I get to tell someone about Jesus, because *then* it will be out of a love relationship with the Lord that has filled me to overflowing and my flesh is dead. I am saying no to the three distractions that come against me, and I am saying yes to Him. The world doesn't need my opinions; it doesn't need my way of doing things or my religion. My ego isn't the hero of the story. There is only One, and His name is Jesus. The world doesn't need more of me; the world needs Jesus. I need Him. You need Him. Just preach Jesus. Just sing Jesus. It is the most beautiful name that could ever come across our lips. He is worthy of our praise.

The Word of God says to us today, "Stand." You may have come through the fire, wind, and rain, and it may feel like hell itself has been unleashed against you. Stand. God has brought you too far to leave you where you are. Stand. You have a divine purpose to fulfill. Stand. God has chosen you for such a time as this. Stand. You haven't even scratched the surface of God's great plans for your life. Stand.

Yes, people will come against you, and trials will get hotter, but the fire of God's Spirit is much hotter within you than the fire of any trial you will ever face. Stand. How long? Until you accomplish everything God has put you here to do. Stand until you receive everything God has promised you. Stand until you go from desperation to total devotion and reckless abandonment. Stand and expect to see the salvation of the Lord.

We don't have to know much; we just need to know Jesus, and He will do the rest. Just get to know Him. Daily seek His face. My prayer is that this Bible study wasn't just an emotional experience but that you now *know* Jesus. Whether it is the first time you have ever met Him, the first time you have ever seen and sought His face above His hand, or if you have returned to your First Love. Whatever that may look like for you, I pray it is based and rooted in the truth of the Word, of who Jesus is, not in an emotional experience. We may be coming to the end of *Wanted*, but it's only the start of the journey of walking in the abundant life, living hand

in hand with Jesus Christ, knowing *whose* you are, and inviting others to come and meet the One who knows all about you and *still wanted you.*

I am my beloved's, and his desire is toward me. (Song of Solomon 7:10)

Come, see a man, which told me all things that ever I did: is not this the Christ? (John 4:29)

GROUP DISCUSSION QUESTIONS

So, Now What?

How do you feel when your read 1 Corinthians 6:15–20? Do you believe we are either a devoted bride or a distracted harlot? Why or why not?

_____

_____

_____

_____

_____

_____

What are some things that are keeping you from "attending upon the Lord? (1 Corinthians 7:35)?

_____

_____

_____

_____

_____

_____

Seeing that Satan doesn't use any new tactics since the beginning, what are some of the scriptures you can use against the weapons of mass distraction that will try to keep your eyes from Jesus?

_____

_____

_____

_____

_____

_____

What comes to mind knowing Jesus desires to hear your voice and see your face? Do you desire to see and hear from Him? Why or why not (Song of Solomon 2:14)?

_____

_____

_____

_____

_____

_____

Describe what it means to you to know that if you seek the face of Jesus first, He will handle everything else in your life. What are some scriptures to support this truth?

_____

_____

_____

_____

_____

_____

CHAPTER 12

PRAYING THE SCRIPTURE THROUGH

the study

The Lord is nigh unto all them that call upon him, to all that call upon him in truth. (Psalm 145:18)

Sanctify them through thy truth: thy word is truth. (John 17:17)

And this is the confidence that we have in him, that, if we ask anything according to his will, he heareth us: and if we know that he hear us, whatsoever we ask, we know that we have the petitions that we desired of him. (1 John 5:14–15)

Scripture-based prayer isn't an invention or formula of mankind, but it is how the Lord wants us to pray. The Bible says we can have confidence that He not only hears us but will answer our prayers if we pray according to His will. Well, how do we pray His will? How do we know what is on His mind?

Let this mind be in you, which is also in Christ Jesus. (Philippians 2:5)

If ye abide in me, and my words abide in you, ye shall ask what ye will, and it shall be done unto you. (John 15:7)

Let the word of Christ dwell in you richly in all wisdom; teaching and admonishing one another in psalms and hymns and spiritual songs, singing with grace in your hearts to the Lord. (Colossians 3:16)

By being in the Word and praying the Word back to Him, by getting to *know* Jesus, we know what His will is. We cannot get to know someone without spending time with him or her. By seeking His face, not just what He can do or give us, our hearts conform to His heart. Our minds transform into His mind. The more we know Him, the more we long for what He wants, His will; therefore, our prayers become aligned with His Word, which is His will, and we can confidently say that we know He hears us and will answer. Our prayer life changes from "God, will You … ?" to "God You are … !" And that, my friend, changes everything about anything.

In the following pages, you will find sample prayers using the scriptures throughout this study. I encourage you to give them a try. You won't regret it.

INTRODUCTION AND THE WORD, THE WELL, AND THE WOMAN

I am my beloved's, and his desire is toward me. (Song of Solomon 7:10)

Lord Jesus, the fact that You want me leaves me in awe of You and Your love. You not only want me, but You changed my name, my title, my label to Yours … Beloved. I praise You and thank You for all You have done for me to make a way so I could get to know You personally and intimately. Help me not to take You for granted but to seek You in all I do with every breath I breathe. In Jesus's name.

> Love not the world, neither the things that are in the world. If any man love the world, the love of the Father is not in him. (1 John 2:15)

Lord Jesus, You are the Lord of all creation, of heaven and earth. All things are under You and Your authority. You are also love. You, Jesus, are the face of love … I simply ask that You would help me to love You and not the world, that my heart would be fixed on Your face and love what You love, nothing more and nothing less. Continue to change my heart as You continue to wash and transform my mind to mimic Yours. Help me to be ready to choose You over everything this world has to offer me, because You are the only One who satisfies. You are enough for me. In Jesus's name.

> For the Son of man is come to seek and to save that which was lost. (Luke 19:10)

Lord Jesus, You are the Son of God and Son of Man. You are the face of the one true God. My words will fail to express the thankfulness and gratitude I have knowing You came to seek what was lost in the garden, an intimate relationship with You. Thank You for desiring a relationship with me and for providing the way for me to have one. All I have to do is believe You are the Son of God, that You paid my sin debt on the cross, and that You rose out of that grave three days later and now sit at the right hand of the Father. Thank You for coming to where I was and offering me this precious gift of knowing You. I have never regretted saying yes to You. I love You, Jesus!

> He that hath the bride is the bridegroom: but the friend of the bridegroom, which standeth and heareth him, rejoiceth greatly because of the bridegroom's voice: this my joy therefore is fulfilled. (John 3:29)

Lord Jesus, You are the soon-coming King and my Bridegroom. I am so thankful that You have me and that I have You. I am so thankful for the Holy Spirit You have given to me, not only

to teach and guide me through this life but also to remind me every day of Your love toward me and of Your promise that You are coming soon to carry me home to forever be with You. I cannot wait to see Your face and hear Your voice. Until then, Jesus, help me to stay faithful and live this life in a way that is pleasing to You. In Jesus's name.

THE ENCOUNTER

> There cometh a woman of Samaria to draw water: Jesus saith unto her, Give me to drink. (John 4:7)

Lord Jesus, I cannot find the words to thank You for Your love. You are God. You are Savior. And You came. You could have demanded that we come to You, but You came to us. You came to me right where I was, and You spoke first. Thank You. I have no other words to say, so let my life reflect my thankfulness to You. Help me to love You with the same love You show me every day. I want to fall more in love with you with every heartbeat. I love You so much. In Jesus's name.

> Wherefore seeing we also are compassed about with so great a cloud of witnesses, let us lay aside every weight, and the sin which doth so easily beset us, and let us run with patience the race that is set before us, looking unto Jesus the author and finisher of our faith; who for the joy that was set before him endured the cross, despising the shame, and is set down at the right hand of the throne of God. (Hebrews 12:1–2)

Lord Jesus, I thank You for Your Word. I thank You that You have written down and preserved throughout the ages these examples of what it means to worship You in obedience to You. Lord, just as the woman at the well left her waterpot after her encounter with You, may I also leave my waterpot, the sin that is heavy, the weight of guilt and shame, and may I run after You. And as I seek Your face to know You more and more, may I not be ashamed to boldly tell everyone who will listen about who You are. May my life draw men and women to You because You are high and lifted up in all I do and say. In Jesus's name.

> Then I will sprinkle clean water upon you, and ye shall be clean: from all your filthiness, and from all your idols, will I cleanse you. A new heart also will I give you, and a new spirit will I put within you: and I will take away the stony heart out of your flesh, and I will give you an heart of flesh. And I will put my spirit within you, and cause you to walk in my statutes, and ye shall keep my judgments, and do them. (Ezekiel 36:25–27)

Lord Jesus, You are the One who makes all things new. You are the One who washes us clean from the filth of this world and of my sins with the truth of Your Word. You are the One who has taken my bitter, angry, and selfish heart, and given me Your heart, which beats for You through the power of Your Holy Spirit and the Word. Thank You for wanting to walk with me during the rest of my days on this earth and into a glorious eternity with You. Give me the passion and boldness to tell others of You so they may also know and love You. In Jesus's name.

THE TEMPLE

What? know ye not that your body is the temple of the Holy Ghost which is in you, which ye have of God, and ye are not your own? For ye are bought with a price: therefore glorify God in your body, and in your spirit, which are God's. (1 Corinthians 6:19–20)

Lord Jesus, once again I am left in awe of You. You, the Holy God, want me and desire to dwell within me. Lord, help me not to rush through this beautiful truth. The glory that filled the tabernacle, that caused every man to fall to his or her face, is the same glory that fills me. Lord, open my heart, mind, and eyes to see the gravity of this. Lord, may I be so bold as to ask that You shake me of everything that pollutes Your temple and give me the courage and the love for You to want to quickly get rid of it, no matter what it is. That isn't an easy thing to ask, but Lord, may I love You more than anything You will expose, simply because You are worth it all. In Jesus's name.

Even them will I bring to my holy mountain, and make them joyful in my house of prayer: their burnt-offerings and their sacrifices shall be accepted upon mine altar; for mine house shall be called an house of prayer for all people. (Isaiah 56:7)

Lord Jesus, I praise You for being the God who loves and gives us all a chance to know You personally because You want to have a relationship with us. You speak through Your Word and have given us a way to speak to You in prayer. Lord, may You be the first One I want to talk to when I wake up and the last I want to hear from before I fall asleep; cultivate a longing to be in constant communication with You through the Word and prayer every waking moment and in between. Hide Your Word in my heart, Jesus. Help me to cling to all of it, so this life is honoring to You as I walk with You each day. I love You, Jesus. May You be praised in and through this earthen vessel, my body, in Jesus's name.

Oh my dove, that are in the clefts of the rock, in the secret places of the stairs, let me see thy countenance, let me hear thy voice; for sweet is thy voice, and thy countenance is comely. (Song of Solomon 2:14)

Lord Jesus, how You have swept me off my feet with this truth of how You think of me. You *want* to hear my voice. You *want* to see my face. You *want* to spend time with me. You long for me to look on You as You look on me. You call me "beautiful" and say our conversation is sweet. Continue to fan within me a passion for You, Jesus. May I love You with reckless abandon, just as You love me. Lord, You have left me breathless and in awe. You are beautiful, and there is nothing and no one I want more than You. I love You, Jesus.

W: WATER

> For I have satiated the weary soul, and I have replenished every sorrowful soul. (Jeremiah 31:25)

Lord Jesus, You are enough. You are all in all. You are everything. You are the only One who can satisfy to overflowing. I know this because I have tasted and seen this in my life. You have filled my weary soul with You, and You have given to me what was lost, a personal relationship with You. You, Jesus, have taken my sorrowful soul and have become my joy, hope, and peace. Only You can do this, and You have done this for me. Oh, how I praise You for restoring me, Jesus, according to Your Word! There is nothing greater than knowing You and being known by You. Help me to live this day by faithfully worshipping You in all I do. In Jesus's name.

> Then washed I thee with water; yea, I throughly washed away thy blood from thee, and I anointed thee with oil. (Ezekiel 16:9)

Lord Jesus, I thank You for Your loving-kindness. I thank You that Your Word, which is You, washes away my sin … all of it. I thank You that You have made a way to daily cleanse me from the filth of the world I come in contact with, and I thank You that Your Word also washes away the daily sins I allow into this temple. Help me to always turn to Your Word for encouragement, help, and cleansing. Lord, You are so good, and Your mercy endures forever.

> And to know the love of Christ, which passeth knowledge, that ye might be filled with all the fullness of God. (Ephesians 3:19)

Lord Jesus, I want to know You. To know You is to love You. To love You is to crave You. To crave You is to live in relentless pursuit of You. I just want You! Knowing You truly fills me to overflowing. I cannot contain Your love, joy, hope, forgiveness, and grace. I cannot help but want to tell others of who You are and all You have done. My desire is to never get over You and to always make it all about You. You are worthy of it all.

A: ADORN

Blessed be the Lord God of our fathers, which hath put such a thing as this in the king's heart, to beautify the house of the Lord which is in Jerusalem. (Ezra 7:27)

Lord Jesus, I bless You. I praise You, because You are good. You are wonderful and beautiful. I thank You that You are the One who changes hearts and the desires of the heart. Thank You for placing in me the desire to make this temple beautiful, to make it ready, as a bride for her bridegroom. Continue to reveal to me what all needs to be removed and what all needs to be added to my life, to this body, to make it ready and beautiful in Your eyes, Jesus. Help me to allow You to have the leadership, the throne, in my life; and to follow You as You prepare me for our wedding day. I cannot wait to see You face-to-face. I love You so much!

> Christ hath redeemed us from the curse of the law, being made a curse for us: for it is written, Cursed is every one that hangeth on a tree: that the blessing of Abraham might come on the Gentiles through Jesus Christ; that we might receive the promise of the Spirit through faith. (Galatians 3:13–14)

Lord Jesus, You are the Lamb of God. That isn't just a title; it is what You are. You were the perfect sacrifice, You endured the wrath of God so that I could know You and have the promise to live with You for all eternity. May I never forget what You did, the price that was paid for my debt. Your love, Lord, has overwhelmed me. As You continue to expose what corrupts my temple, in those moments when it's hard and painful to crucify my flesh, may I remember what You did for me, because I know that when I remember the price You paid for me, I will gladly surrender whatever it is You are asking me to lay down. Precious Jesus, thank You so much for loving me *this much*. Help me to love You with the same sacrificial love You give to me. In Jesus's name.

> And he answered and spake unto those that stood before him, saying, Take away the filthy garments from him. And unto him he said, Behold, I have caused thine iniquity to pass from thee, and I will clothe thee with change of raiment. (Zechariah 3:4)

Lord Jesus, I thank You that You are the One who speaks. You speak not only to us but also on our behalf. I thank You that You are the One who stands between me and my accusers. You are the Lord who fights our battles, and Your truth silences the lies. You, Lord, knew the garments I was in when You found me, yet You still offered me Your robe, Your garment, in exchange for the filthy rags of wickedness, evil, darkness, and sin. I will never understand why You love me so much, but oh, how thankful I am that You do. You leave me undone, Jesus! Help me to live a life worthy of the robe You have placed on me. In Jesus's name.

N: NURTURE

My voice shalt thou hear in the morning, O Lord; in the morning will I direct
my prayer unto thee, and will look up. (Psalm 5:3)

Lord Jesus, You are the First and the Last, the Beginning and the End. I pray that will be said
of You in my personal life—that when I wake up, You are the first of my thoughts; that You
are the beginning of my day; that my heart will long for You before anything and anyone else;
and that I will be in a hurry to meet with You, sit at Your feet, and hear what You have to say.
And I pray that at the end of the day, You will be the last thing on my mind, that my heart will
be longing and dwelling on You. This is my heart's desire, Lord. Help me to look up always,
to seek You. In Jesus's name.

> Then Jesus said unto them, Verily, verily, I say unto you, Moses gave you
> not that bread from heaven; but my Father giveth you the true bread from
> heaven. For the bread of God is he which cometh down from heaven, and
> giveth life unto the world. Then said they unto him, Lord, evermore give us
> this bread. And Jesus said unto them, I am the bread of life: he that cometh
> to me shall never hunger; and he that believeth on me shall never thirst.
> (John 6:32–35)

Lord Jesus, You are the Bread of Life, the Bread sent from heaven. Thank You for coming.
You didn't have to, but You did. You satisfy every longing of my heart and of my body. You,
the Word, have the power to sustain me physically, mentally, emotionally, and spiritually.
You are truly everything I will ever need and everything I could ever want. It is all wrapped
up in You, Jesus. Thank You for allowing me this precious gift of knowing You and living a
life of complete and total satisfaction that exists only in, with, through, and by You … the
Word … my Beloved.

> Thy words were found, and I did eat them; and thy word was unto me the joy
> and rejoicing of mine heart: for I am called by thy name, O Lord God of hosts.
> (Jeremiah 15:16)

Lord Jesus, You came. You were found because You came. You are truth, and You speak truth,
giving us a chance to hear, to allow it to soak into our hearts and minds. And as we take it all
in, Your Word becomes what gives us joy—not just happiness but a pure, true, deep-seeded
joy that cannot be shaken. Not in pain, not in distress, not in the trying of our faith. Nothing,
Lord, can shake or take away the joy of You within me. Your Word causes me to rejoice, even
when it doesn't make sense to the world. That is what You do in me. You have changed me from

darkness to light, condemned to forgiven, forsaken to beloved. You have given me Your name, so I will praise You in the storm. I will praise You in the fire. I will praise You in the shaking of everything around me. I will praise You because You are the joy of my soul, the love of my life, and the peace of my heart. And You are worthy to be praised.

T: TEACH

> That the trial of your faith, being much more precious than of gold that perisheth, though it be tried with fire, might be found unto praise and honour and glory at the appearing of Jesus Christ. (1 Peter 1:7)

Lord Jesus, You are the victorious soon-coming King of king and Lord of lords. You are the God who keeps His Word, and You promise that You are coming for Your bride and to make all things right. May I not lose sight of that truth, Jesus. May my eyes be fixed on Your face and my heart set on Your glorious appearing. Until then, Lord, Your Word says my faith will be tried by fire. Help me to remember You are the Man in the fire; You will remain there with me through every trial and testing of faith just so I know I'm not alone. And help me to see that these moments, though painful and uncomfortable, are for Your glory. And if it is for Your glory that they will always be for my good. Help me to stay in You, in Your Word, Jesus, through it all. In Jesus's name.

> Examine me, O Lord, and prove me; try my reins and my heart. For thy lovingkindness is before mine eyes: and I have walked in thy truth. (Psalm 26:2–3)

Lord Jesus, You are Lord. You are the One who created everything, and You are the One who has the right to declare what is good and what is evil. With a trembling heart, I ask You to examine me according to Your standard, not mine nor the world's. In Thy loving-kindness, You are before my eyes as I seek Your face, and I just want to please You; to do so is to walk in Your way, truth, and life. May I put a smile on Your face, Lord. You are the only One worth living for, and You are the only One whose opinion matters to me. Oh, how I love You! Help me to fall more in love with each breath I take. In Jesus's name.

> Before I was afflicted I went astray: but now have I kept thy word … It is good for me that I have been afflicted; that I might learn thy statutes. (Psalm 119:67, 71)

Lord Jesus, I thank You that You love me enough to correct me when I'm living a life that doesn't glorify You. I thank You that You want me to live an abundant life in You to the point that You will afflict me however You see fit to keep me from falling from the straight and narrow path You have designed for me to walk. Thank You that even in Your correction, though uncomfortable and painful, there is an undeniable love and compassion toward me. Help me not to resist You during these times and help me to remember that this is for Your glory, my good, and the purpose of knowing You more. Your love, Lord—there are no words in this human language that could begin to express what it means to me. Thank You for loving me, Jesus. Thank You with all my heart.

E: EMPOWER

> I know thy works, and thy labour, and thy patience, and how thou canst not bear them which are evil: and thou hast tried them which say they are apostles, and are not, and hast found them liars: … Nevertheless I have somewhat against thee, because thou hast left thy first love. (Revelation 2:2, 4)

Lord Jesus, I praise You that You know, that You pay attention to, what we do including the intents of our hearts. That only proves You are a personal, hands-on God. You are concerned with what takes place in our lives and what we are part of. Lord, You also know that my mind and heart can be more focused on the calling of my life and stray from You. I can so easily fall in love with what You have given me that I forsake You. Lord, I know I have been unfaithful to You and have made the talents and gifts You have given me my idols. Forgive me, Jesus, for cheating on You. Help me to keep and guard my heart with Your Word, to love You only, and to desire and long for the Giver above the gift. My heart is prone to wander, but Your Word says what I see affects my heart, so help me to always seek Your face, to behold Your glory and beauty always. In Jesus's name.

> For the time will come when they will not endure sound doctrine; but after their own lusts shall they heap to themselves teachers, having itching ears; and they shall turn away their ears from the truth, and shall be turned unto fables. (2 Timothy 4:3–4)

Lord Jesus, You are the truth. There is no false way in You or about You. You cannot lie. It isn't that You choose not to lie; You simply can't. For that, Jesus, I praise You. I can trust You and Your Word above any other. It is in this understanding of who You are that I not only focus on You but also live a life that points others to You. My flesh will want the glory, praise, and applause of others. Lord, help me to crucify my flesh so You live through me and Your name is

lifted high, so Your face is seen, so Your glory is experienced, and so others will be encouraged by You. May they be strengthened by You, have an encounter with You, and come to know You. This life has nothing to do with me, and that is what the world is centered on, making it all about "self." But this life has everything to do with You. I am desperate for You to take over and do Your will in and through my life, even if it goes against what everyone else around me believes. In Jesus's name.

> When thou saidst, Seek ye my face; my heart said unto thee, Thy face, Lord, will I seek. (Psalm 27:8)

Lord Jesus, You are the only One worth knowing. The more I know You, the more I love You. The more I love You, the more of You I want, and the closer I want to be to You. I cannot get enough of You, yet You leave me filled and satisfied. I don't know how You do that, but You do. You are the longing of my heart. You are the love of my life. You are everything to me, and You are enough. Keep my eyes on You, Jesus. Keep me focused on You. May Your Word be all I hear! You are the Author and Finisher of my faith. Help me to always choose You above all others, including myself. Oh, I am so in love with You. May Your love be what fuels me to love You more with all I am, all I have, because You are worthy of it all.

D: DELIVER

> Let my supplication come before thee: deliver me according to thy word. (Psalm 119:170)

Lord Jesus, You are the God who hears. You want to hear from me. And even though You already know the outcome, You want to be with us in the moment and care for us. Thank You that You are approachable. As I face the struggles and problems of life, whether they are things of my past trying to convince me that I am not who You say I am, current battles or temptations remind me that You are the Deliverer of my soul. And if You have the power to deliver my soul from hell, then there is nothing I'm going through that You cannot deliver me from. Help me to trust in Your timing and purposes through it all. You are the Deliverer, and You will deliver me for Your glory, honor, and praise.

> Then said Jesus to those Jews which believed on him, If ye continue in my word, then are ye my disciples indeed; and ye shall know the truth, and the truth shall make you free. (John 8:31–32)

Lord Jesus, You are the Word. I thank You for making a way for me to know You and providing a way for me to continue in You … in Spirit and truth. And You, Jesus, make me free. You don't just *set* me free; You *make* me free. Being made free is a newness of life, a new beginning, a changing of everything. In Your freedom, my thinking changes, my heart's desire changes, my purpose changes, and my reason for every breath changes. It changes from a life based on my wants and understanding to a life centered on You with a desire to know and love You, to proclaim Your goodness to others so they can know You and love You. It's time now to bring You honor, glory, praise, and blessing; to worship You as a faithful, surrendered, willing servant. Your blood paid the way for my freedom. For that alone, Jesus, I am all Yours. I am all in. Take over! I surrender all of me to You. It is an honor and joy to do so.

> I waited patiently for the Lord; and he inclined unto me, and heard my cry. He brought me up also out of an horrible pit, out of the miry clay, and set my feet upon a rock, and established my goings. And he hath put a new song in my mouth, even praise unto our God: many shall see it, and fear, and shall trust in the Lord. (Psalm 40:1–3)

Lord Jesus, You are the keeper of time. Because Your timing is perfect, help me to wait patiently for You and for Your Word to be fulfilled in my life. Help me to trust that You hear me, that I am not forgotten or ignored by You. You have a divine purpose and plan, and I can trust Your timing. I have experienced Your plucking me up from a horrible pit and the heavy, miry clay. You set me on a rock, on a higher place; therefore, I will trust that You will do the same in every situation. While in the waiting, help me to sing to You. Help me to praise You louder than I would if I were on the mountaintop. Here is where it counts. Here is where the world is watching. And it is this new song You have given me before the deliverance, that will cause many to pay attention. It is this song that will cause darkness itself to tremble. It is this song that will draw many to You, and they will come to know and trust You for themselves. So help me to sing to You now when it is hard and painful, when it is truly a sacrifice of praise simply because You are worthy. You are good, and Your mercy endures forever.

ABOUT THE AUTHOR

Angela is the oldest of four daughters born to Bobby and Becky Bonner. Bobby Bonner played professional baseball for the Baltimore Orioles, but at the age of 28, walked away from "The Show" and answered the call to be a missionary to Zambia, Africa

Angela was born again, August of 2003, when Jesus "must needs go through" her living room in Katy, TX, where she met her Lord and Savior and she hasn't gotten over Him!

Angela's life verse is Philippians 1:20-21 "According to my earnest expectation and my hope, that in nothing I shall be ashamed, but that with all boldness, as always, so now also Christ shall be magnified in my body, whether it be by life or by death. For to me to live is Christ, and to die is gain." Life has not been easy, but Angela would tell you that every tear, every trial, every pain was worth it all. She will tell you "Because it was in those times I got to know my Savior more. To know Him and to be known by Him is the greatest treasure of my life. He is my everything."

Angela is this century's "woman at the well." She left her "waterpot", the weight of her past at His feet and is STILL running, saying "COME! COME and see the One Who knew everything about me and still wanted me! He is the Christ! You have got to KNOW HIM!"

Angela and her husband, Micheal, are native Texans, with three children and two grandchildren. They moved to Decatur, AL in 2012 with their two boys and are members of Decatur Baptist Church and is part of the worship team, helps lead in the prayer movement at her church, teaches and speaks at women's events, and enjoys getting to know her Jesus more with every Bible study He leads her to write.

REFERENCES

1   *Webster's Dictionary 1828*, s.v. "betroth," accessed June 2, 2012, https://webstersdictionary1828.com/Dictionary/Betroth

2   *Strong's Greek Lexicon (kjv)*, s.v. "G1163-dei," accessed June 2, 2012, https://www.blueletterbible.org/lexicon/g1163/kjv/tr/ss1/0-1/

3   *Webster's Dictionary 1828*, s.v. "know," accessed June 2, 2012, https://webstersdictionary1828.com/Dictionary/Know

4   *Webster's Dictionary 1828, s.v. "intimate," accessed June 2, 2012, https://webstersdictionary1828.com/Dictionary/Intimate*

5   *Webster's Dictionary 1828*, s.v. "sealed," accessed June 2, 2012, https://webstersdictionary1828.com/Dictionary/Sealed

6   *Webster's Dictionary 1828*, s.v. "covenant," accessed June 8, 2012, https://webstersdictionary1828.com/Dictionary/Covenant

7   *Webster's Dictionary 1828*, s.v. "satiate," accessed September 8, 2012, https://webstersdictionary1828.com/Dictionary/Satiate

8   *Webster's Dictionary 1828*, s.v. "abound," accessed September 8, 2012, https://webstersdictionary1828.com/Dictionary/Abound

9   *Webster's Dictionary 1828*, s.v. "choice," accessed September 10, 2012, https://webstersdictionary1828.com/Dictionary/Choice

10 *Webster's Dictionary 1828*, s.v. "comeliness," accessed October 1, 2012, https://webstersdictionary1828.com/Dictionary/Comeliness

11 *Webster's Dictionary 1828*, s.v. "blessed," accessed October 1, 2012, https://webstersdictionary1828.com/Dictionary/Blessed

12 *Webster's Dictionary 1828*, s.v. "cursed," accessed October 2, 2012, https://webstersdictionary1828.com/Dictionary/Cursed

13 *Webster's Dictionary 1828*, s.v. "nurture," accessed October 28, 2012, https://webstersdictionary1828.com/Dictionary/Nurture

14 *Webster's Dictionary 1828*, s.v. "apathetic," accessed November 18, 2012, https://webstersdictionary1828.com/Dictionary/Apathetic

15 *Merriam-Webster.com Dictionary*, s.v. "teach," accessed November 18, 2012, https://www.merriam-webster.com/dictionary/teach

16 *Strong's Greek Lexicon (kjv),* s.v. "G1381-dokimazo," accessed November 19, 2012, https://www.blueletterbible.org/lexicon/g1381/kjv/tr/0-1/

17 *Strong's Greek Lexicon (kjv),* s.v. "G1411-dunamis," accessed December 4, 2012, https://www.blueletterbible.org/lexicon/g1411/kjv/tr/0-1/

18 *Webster's Dictionary 1828*, s.v. "covetous," accessed March 3, 2013, https://webstersdictionary1828.com/Dictionary/Covetous

19 *Webster's Dictionary 1828*, s.v. "boaster," accessed March 3, 2013, https://webstersdictionary1828.com/Dictionary/Boaster

20 *Webster's Dictionary 1828*, s.v. "blasphemer," accessed March 3, 2013, https://webstersdictionary1828.com/Dictionary/Blasphemer

21 *Webster's Dictionary 1828*, s.v. "truce-breaker," accessed March 3, 2013, https://webstersdictionary1828.com/Dictionary/Truce-breaker

22 *Webster's Dictionary 1828*, s.v. "incontinent," accessed March 3, 2013, https://webstersdictionary1828.com/Dictionary/Incontinent

23 *Webster's Dictionary 1828*, s.v. "fierce," accessed March 3, 2013, https://webstersdictionary1828.com/Dictionary/Fierce

24 *Webster's Dictionary 1828*, s.v. "traitor," accessed March 3, 2013, https://webstersdictionary1828.com/Dictionary/Traitor

25 *Webster's Dictionary 1828*, s.v. "heady," accessed March 3, 2013, https://webstersdictionary1828.com/Dictionary/Heady

26 *Webster's Dictionary 1828*, s.v. "high-minded," accessed March 3, 2013, https://webstersdictonary1828.com/Dictionary/High-minded

27 *Webster's Dictionary 1828*, s.v. "astonish," accessed April 8, 2013, https://webstersdictionary1828.com/Dictionary/Astonish

28 *Webster's Dictionary 1828*, s.v. "deliver," accessed July 3, 2013, https://webstersdictionary1828.com/Dictionary/Deliver

29 *Webster's Dictionary 1828*, s.v. "attend," accessed August 16, 2013, https://webstersdictionary1828.com/Dictionary/Attend

30 *Webster's Dictionary 1828*, s.v. "beguile," accessed August 16, 2013, https://webstersdictionary1828.com/Dictionary/Beguile

31 *Webster's Dictionary 1828*, s.v. "harlot," accessed August 16, 2013, https://webstersdictionary1828.com/Dictionary/Harlot

inted in the United States
Baker & Taylor Publisher Services